Studies in Parapsychology

Volumes in the Collier Books Edition of
The Collected Papers of Sigmund Freud

Each volume has an Introduction by the Editor,
Philip Rieff.

Studies in Parapsychology

SIGMUND FREUD

WITH AN INTRODUCTION BY THE EDITOR

PHILIP RIEFF

COLLIER BOOKS
Macmillan Publishing Company
NEW YORK

Macmillan Publishing Company,
866 Third Avenue,
New York, N.Y. 10022.

This Collier Books edition is published by arrangement with Basic Books, Inc.

Library of Congress Catalog Card Number: 63-14965.

First Collier Books Edition 1963

ISBN: 0-02-076550-9

10   9   8   7   6

Macmillan books are available at special discounts for bulk purchases for sales promotions, premiums, fund-raising, or educational use. For details, contact:

> Special Sales Director
> Macmillan Publishing Company
> 866 Third Avenue
> New York, N.Y. 10022

Printed in the United States of America

Contents

Introduction

THERE ARE NO easy triumphs in the world of the intellect. Freud's essay on "The Uncanny" is an outstanding example of the fact that, though he became the intellectual master of our age, his was not an effortless mastery. Freud worked hard—on himself, and at his writing. Thus, a minor triumph, "The Uncanny," lay in his drawer from the unknown date of its first drafting until the month of May, 1919, when he dug it out for rewriting. The essay lay waiting an interpretative category that would give it life and coherence.

It appears likely that, while working on *Beyond the Pleasure Principle,* Freud turned back to "The Uncanny" and transferred to that essay, earlier conceived, a vital idea from the later work. In the famous "compulsion to repeat," Freud found the concept that was to give unity and truth to an essay which, without such a transfusion of theory, would have remained a relatively pale piece of erudition about problems that had long embarrassed both science and art—eerie feelings, premonitions, telepathic communications, terrifying fantasies and the like.

Freud's explanation of the whole range of the uncanny has never been bettered. In default of serious competing theories, we will have to be satisfied with the idea that the uncanny is "something which is secretly familiar, which has undergone repression and then returned from it. . . . Everything that is uncanny fulfills this condition . . . [although] not everything that fulfills this condition . . . is on that account uncanny."

All of Freud's best writing has a certain tension, a reaching out for that which is just beyond reach—more precisely, an effort to say something not yet said, by fusing data all too familiar (and therefore a little contemptible) with an unfamiliar theory. The effect is rather uncanny. And not a few readers have this feeling of something uncanny in reading the work of a powerful mind capable of "laying bare . . . hidden forces," as Freud himself noticed. The reader comes to a work with ambivalent motives, learning what he does not wish to know, or, what amounts to the same thing, believing he already knows and can accept as his own intellectual property what the author merely "articulates" or "expresses" for him. Of course, in this sense, everybody knows everything—or nobody could learn anything. The effect of every first-rate piece of writing is to combine the familiar with the unfamiliar. Freud's genius was not really in the discovery of new facts but rather in the supplying of new perspectives on old and often disused facts, such as those upon which shamans, quacks, mediums and mystics have based modes of knowing outside the respectable precincts of our rationalist culture. It is, thus, as a *theoretician* rather than an *empirical* research worker that his genius persists.

Freud was a rare rationalist, one who respected the irrational. In his intuition of the unity of truth, he leaped upon all manner of experience, even those dismissed as false and fraudulent by minds with lesser capacities to entertain the conceptual unities that are the constituent truths of the worlds of both science and art. It is at this point, indeed, that intellectual certainty, the only substitute for anti-intellectual faith, is achieved, through the fusion of analytic and aesthetic capacities. Freud was able to fuse these capacities. He was gifted with a sense of intellectual certainty, of the sort every scientist and artist needs. But for this sense of certainty he often has been blamed, as if this sense is not the cost of every creative act.

Having found his own mode of certainty, Freud had the courage to let it lead him into jurisdictions where he would not otherwise have entered. These essays are far from the main lines of psychoanalytic investigation. Yet, given the intellectual weapons with which he was gifted, Freud made incursions into the field of parapsychology, which is even more remote from the settled credulities of science and common sense than infantile sexuality is from that of theology and moral sentiment.

In these essays Freud is intent on breaking the hold of the "omnipotence of thought" over those areas of experience that are the investigative jurisdictions, nowadays, of the parapsychologist. Being a psychoanalytic rationalist, he knows the limits of the power of consciousness. It is a limit that Rationalism itself has been reluctant to accept; what, then, can be expected of Irrationalist doctrines? All doctrines of the irrational are essentially in praise of the unconscious, asserting the power of that level of mind even over matter. Freud belonged to the skeptical majority, of which I, too, am a member. Those of us who have directed our wills, with only random success, upon the required number in a game of cards, or with equal futility, diffused more mental than physical english over a pool table, know how powerless mind remains over matter. We await a theory that, by freeing the will, pockets the ball. Until that millennial time, the "omnipotence of thought" remains for most of us moderns a merely psychical reality, the stuff of neurotic fantasy, eerie fiction and occult rackets. The mind cannot, upon Freudian or other rationalist hypotheses, act volitionally upon, say, falling dice. Such volitional possibilities, still devoutly wished by some and patiently investigated by others, would revolutionize our pleasures. But, then, I remember: nowadays no revolution can be good. Caught between an inadequately trained consciousness and an untrainable unconscious, our pleasures have a poor prognosis—dying things—like flesh.

Among its more extreme proponents, parapsychology is a kind of religion, and, indeed, raises the same ultimate promise as our historic Western religions: that, after all, we never quite die. Yet, from the evidence adduced, survival after death promises a boring time. Even the great late psychical researcher, F. W. H. Myers, in that part of his personality which (he thought) might retain the capacity to enter the minds of others, could, according to the most devoted witnesses of his re-entry,

only express his old academic passion for classical literature; surely it would have been preferable that he remain
forever silent. Myers had his say, at Cambridge and in
books, when his personality was incarnate. Nobody has
a supernatural right to go on talking shop from the Beyond,
as if he were eternally at a faculty party. There is too much
talk in the world as it is; a science that would allow the
dead merely to repeat themselves can hold out no hope
for the living. More seriously, I should say that science
has no business being either hopeful or hopeless. A science
of personality disincarnate cannot be concerned with the
question of whether that personality is transformed in
fading away; such transformations are the waking dreams
with which religions have comforted the living, by imagin-
ing something better than life itself. On the evidence thus
far, death has no meaning, except as it is a projective
symbolism expressing the fears and hopes of the living.

As a psychoanalyst, in these essays Freud reviews some
of the problems of parapsychology. Sociologists must fear
even to look in the direction Freud thus took occasionally.
The departmental gods will be offended. But it is not taboo
to be reminded by other worlds of one's own. In reading
psychical research reports, I am often reminded of an area
over which sociology now rules: religious behavior. (Sociology picks up subjects by default, the psychologists having abandoned this one as less amenable than pigeon
behavior to their rigorous testing devices.) There appears
a remarkable uniformity in the way extrasensory knowledge is acquired, and, moreover, a remarkable similarity
in the attitude of percipients. These extraordinary ways
of knowing would appear, to a sociologist, as secular
modes of what used to be called "mystical understanding."

Although it will not please theologians to think so, religion has been one major way in which people have saved
themselves from the strain of excessive intellectualism.
Reason cannot do everything. Since the eighteenth century,
the long supremacy of intellect has been undercut not least
by the rationalists themselves. Finally, with Freud, at
least in the first two stages of his intellectual development,

Reason was made a constitutional monarch, charged with the function of appointing ruling parties to office from the parliament of emotions, and occasionally reading out a message on future policy from which that parliament could take its cues for action. But the majesty of Reason now needs all kinds of clever supporting publicity; it is no longer divinely ordered or natural, but, rather, a therapeutic fiction.

Mystics, not only of western but even more emphatically of oriental traditions, were never much impressed with either the majesty or power of Reason. On the contrary, of the two types of religion, that generally called mystical is constantly at war with the other, which is intellectual and doctrinal; the second often feeds upon the first, transforming mystical experience into rationalist dogma. Science is the inheritor of the second tradition, specially powerful in the West, almost to the exclusion of mysticism. What was once heresy is now abnormality. Science, equipped with Freudian instruments, is almost ready to pick apart the dynamics of mysticism. But, in this culture, mysticism has never mattered, except as a release from rationally ordered routine. Now, rationalist science, in the shape of depth psychology, pursues the harried, tired old thing to its last hiding place, out beyond the respectable precincts of church and laboratory, into the back rooms where consolations are sold cheaply, mixed with petty shrewdness by mediums with some small gift.

I say "gift" advisedly; the telepath, the clairvoyant, the medium, the automatist have what Gardner Murphy calls a "special gift for the paranormal." That gift consists in relaxing the intellect, almost as in a trance. It is the gift of the religious—or those who, without being aware of their yearning, would be religious if being so did not carry along unbearable institutional restraints.

Parapsychological theory will develop further, I think, when the percipients themselves are more carefully studied from perspectives other than parapsychological. With what questions will they be studied? That Rhine's first and greatest ESP subject, at Duke, was a student in the divinity school, religiously disposed, and from a family apparently so disposed, leads to a sociological question about the transmission of "sick" and "healthy-minded" attitudes. Again, incidents of telepathy are, with significant frequency, as Freud noted, of disasters; this leads to another sociological question. For personalities with mystical inclinations, social life is a sequence of disasters; through their telepathic experience, they perform a therapy of transformation upon their disgust at existence. One of the last of the great American mediums, an old Yankee whom William James used to visit, would put it to James that "the experience of mediumship was a transforming experience in which everything looked different. He looked out, for example, at 'this rusty hayrick,' to which he pointed, and it would become beautiful. It was transformed, took on meaning." Gardner Murphy quotes another person mystically inclined, a Pole who had the "ability . . . to read hidden messages. . . . 'I concentrate, and then in those moments'—here his face was bright with animation—'I become a Christian.' "* The dynamics of personality transformation—whatever the social value attached to such transformations—are better understood than ever before, in part due to the work of Freud. It is difficult to say, however, whether the next advances in understanding can take place strictly within psychology. Perhaps, at the stage to which Freud has helped bring us, historical and sociological analysis will help carry the investigation of parapsychological phenomena further than the psychologists can go on their own. Take, for example, the problem of the decline in the number of first-rate mediums in our culture. The era of great mediums lasted from about 1880 to 1925; this terminal date coincides fairly with the end of the Protestant era. Perhaps survivalist experience was the genteel form of revivalist experience,

* See, for a useful introduction to the problems of parapsychology and psychical research, Gardner Murphy: *Challenge of Psychical Research, A Primer of Parapsychology* (New York, 1961). For a more popular account, see G. H. Estabrooks and N. E. Gross: *The Future of the Human Mind* (New York, 1961).

fit for those rare creatures who could not otherwise express their sense of the over-all meaning of life in a culture
that, in both its waning religious and waxing scientific
phase, denied the legitimacy of mystical modes of understanding.

A telepath "learns" in the same way that a mystic
"knows," with intense emotion and vivid imagery. Both
cherish their private knowledge as an untransferrable
possession—more precisely, as a knowing that has possessed them, relaxed them, and in a historically familiar
way, released them from the rational superficies of everyday life. It may have been this sense of release, so incredible that it had to be believed in, that the residually
religious brought, for examination, to the few investigators
who, like Freud, were interested in so exotic a subject as
feelings of release and possession in a culture that denied
the possibility (and efficacy) of either. In Freudian terms,
the mystic is a vehicle for the expression of feelings that
otherwise must remain repressed, at least in this culture.
But the modern mystic, the telepath, is of a very special,
historical kind: he reports knowledge of evil, terrifying
and out of balance with good. Finally, the events of modern history have emptied out the category of the uncanny.
The repressed has returned, in full vengeance, and therefore repression may no longer be the unit of analysis
upon which to build a psychology of real horror, as con-
trasted with the fictional chills that Freud used for illus-
trative purposes.

PHILIP RIEFF

University of Pennsylvania
1962

Studies in Parapsychology

The "Uncanny" (1919)

I

The "Uncanny"[1] (1919)

1

IT IS ONLY rarely that a psychoanalyst feels impelled to investigate the subject of aesthetics even when aesthetics is understood to mean not merely the theory of beauty, but the theory of the qualities of feeling. He works in other planes of mental life and has little to do with those subdued emotional activities which, inhibited in their aims and dependent upon a multitude of concurrent factors, usually furnish the material for the study of aesthetics. But it does occasionally happen that he has to interest himself in some particular province of that subject; and then it usually proves to be a rather remote region of it and one that has been neglected in standard works.

The subject of the "uncanny" is a province of this kind. It undoubtedly belongs to all that is terrible—to all that arouses dread and creeping horror; it is equally certain, too, that the word is not always used in a clearly definable sense, so that it tends to coincide with whatever excites dread. Yet we may expect that it implies some intrinsic quality which justifies the use of a special name. One is curious to know what this peculiar quality is which allows us to distinguish as "uncanny" certain things within the boundaries of what is "fearful."

As good as nothing is to be found upon this subject in elaborate treatises on aesthetics, which in general prefer to concern themselves with what is beautiful, attractive and sublime, that is with feelings of a positive nature, with the circumstances and the objects that call them forth, rather than with the opposite feelings of unpleasantness

---

[1] First published in *Imago*, Bd. V., 1919; reprinted in *Sammlung*, Fünfte Folge. [Translated by Alix Strachey.]

and repulsion. I know of only one attempt in medico-psychological literature, a fertile but not exhaustive paper by E. Jentsch.[2] But I must confess that I have not made a very thorough examination of the bibliography, especially the foreign literature, relating to this present modest contribution of mine, for reasons which must be obvious at this time;[3] so that my paper is presented to the reader without any claim of priority.

In his study of the "uncanny," Jentsch quite rightly lays stress on the obstacle presented by the fact that people vary so very greatly in their sensitivity to this quality of feeling. The writer of the present contribution, indeed, must himself plead guilty to a special obtuseness in the matter, where extreme delicacy of perception would be more in place. It is long since he has experienced or heard of anything which has given him an uncanny impression, and he will be obliged to translate himself into that state of feeling, and to awaken in himself the possibility of it before he begins. Still, difficulties of this kind make themselves felt powerfully in many other branches of aesthetics; we need not on this account despair of finding instances in which the quality in question will be recognized without hesitation by most people.

Two courses are open to us at the start. Either we can find out what meaning has come to be attached to the word "uncanny" in the course of its history; or we can collect all those properties of persons, things, sensations, experiences and situations which arouse in us the feeling of uncanniness, and then infer the unknown nature of the uncanny from what they all have in common. I will say at once that both courses lead to the same result: the "uncanny" is that class of the terrifying which leads back to something long known to us, once very familiar. How this is possible, in what circumstances the familiar can become uncanny and frightening, I shall show in what

[2] "Zur Psychologie des Unheimlichen."
[3] [An allusion to the European War only just concluded.—Trans.]

follows. Let me also add that my investigation was actually begun by collecting a number of individual cases, and only later received confirmation after I had examined what language could tell us. In this discussion, however, I shall follow the opposite course.

The German word *unheimlich*[4] is obviously the opposite of *heimlich, heimisch,* meaning "familiar," "native," "belonging to the home"; and we are tempted to conclude that what is "uncanny" is frightening precisely because it is *not* known and familiar. Naturally not everything which is new and unfamiliar is frightening, however; the relation cannot be inverted. We can only say that what is novel can easily become frightening and uncanny; some new things are frightening but not by any means all. Something has to be added to what is novel and unfamiliar to make it uncanny.

On the whole, Jentsch did not get beyond this relation of the uncanny to the novel and unfamiliar. He ascribes the essential factor in the production of the feeling of un-canniness to intellectual uncertainty; so that the uncanny would always be that in which one does not know where one is, as it were. The better orientated in his environment a person is, the less readily will he get the impression of something uncanny in regard to the objects and events in it.

It is not difficult to see that this definition is incomplete, and we will therefore try to proceed beyond the equation of *unheimlich* with unfamiliar. We will first turn to other languages. But foreign dictionaries tell us nothing new, perhaps only because we speak a different language. Indeed, we get the impression that many languages are without a word for this particular variety of what is fearful.

I wish to express my indebtedness to Dr. Th. Reik for the following excerpts:

LATIN: (K. E. Georges, *Deutschlateinisches Wörter-buch,* 1898). Ein *unheimlicher* Ort [an uncanny place]

---

[4] [Throughout this paper "uncanny" is used as the English translation of *"unheimlich,"* literally "unhomely."—Trans.]

—locus suspectus; in *unheimlicher* Nachtzeit [in the dismal night hours]—intempesta nocte.

GREEK: (Rost's and Schenkl's Lexikons). *Xenos* strange, foreign.

ENGLISH: (from dictionaries by Lucas, Bellow, Flügel, Muret-Sanders). Uncomfortable, uneasy, gloomy, dismal, uncanny, ghastly; (of a house) haunted; (of a man) a repulsive fellow.

FRENCH: (Sachs-Villatte). Inquiétant, sinistre, lugubre, mal à son aise.

SPANISH: (Tollhausen, 1889). Sospechoso, de mal agüero, lugubre, siniestro.

The Italian and the Portuguese seem to content themselves with words which we should describe as circumlocutions. In Arabic and Hebrew "uncanny" means the same as "daemonic," "gruesome."

Let us therefore return to the German language. In Daniel Sanders' *Wörterbuch der deutschen Sprache* (1860), the following remarks[5] [abstracted in translation]

[5] Vol. i. p. 729. Heimlich, a. (-keit, f. -en): 1. auch Heime-lich, heimelig, zum Hause gehörig, nicht fremd, vertraut, zahm, traut und traulich, anheimelnd etc. (a) (veralt.) zum Haus, zur Familie gehörig, oder: wie dazu gehörig betrachtet, vgl. lat. familiaris, vertraut: Die Heimlichen, die Hausgenossen; Der heimliche Rat. 1. Mos. 41, 45; 2. Sam. 23, 23. 1 Chr. 12, 25. Weish. 8, 4., wofür jetzt: Geheimer (s. d 1.) Rat üblich ist, s. Heimlicher—(b) von Tieren zahm, sich den Menschen traulich anschliessend. Ggstz. wild, z. B. Tier, die weder wild noch heimlich sind, etc. Eppendorf. 88; Wilde Thier . . . so man sie h. und gewohnsam um die Leute auf-zeucht. 92. So diese Thierle von Jugend bei den Menschen erzogen, werden sie ganz h., freundlich etc., Stumpf 608a etc. —So noch: So h. ist's (das Lamm) und frisst aus meiner Hand. Hölty; Ein schöner, heimelicher (s. c) Vogel bleibt der Storch immerhin. Linck, Schl. 146. s. Häuslich. 1 etc.—(c) traut, traulich anheimelnd; das Wohlgefühl stiller Befriedigung etc., behaglicher Ruhe u. sichern Schutzes, wie das um-schlossne wohnliche Haus erregend (vgl. Geheuer): Ist dir's h. noch im Lande, wo die Fremden deine Wälder roden? Alexis H. 1, 1, 289; Es war ihr nicht allzu h. bei ihm. Bren-

THE "UNCANNY" / 23

ire found upon the word *heimlich*; I have laid stress on
certain passages by italicizing them.

Heimlich, adj.: I. Also *heimelich, heimelig*, belonging to the house, not strange, familiar, tame, intimate,
comfortable, homely, etc.

(*a*) (Obsolete) belonging to the house or the family,
or regarded as so belonging (cf. Latin *familiaris*): *Die
Heimlichen*, the members of the household; *Der heimliche Rat* [him to whom secrets are revealed] Gen. xli.
45; 2 Sam. xxiii. 23; now more usually *Geheimer Rat*
[Privy Councillor], cf. *Heimlicher*.

(*b*) Of animals: tame, companionable to man. As
opposed to wild, *e.g.* "Wild animals . . . that are trained
to be *heimlich* and accustomed to men." "If these young
creatures are brought up from early days among men
they become quite *heimlich*, friendly," etc.

(*c*) Friendly, intimate, homelike; the enjoyment of
quiet content, etc., arousing a sense of peaceful pleasure

---

ino Wehm. 92; Auf einem hohen h—en Schattenpfade . . .,
ings dem rieselnden rauschenden und plätschernden Wald-
ach. Forster B. 1, 417. Die H—keit der Heimath zerstören.
iervinus Lit. 5, 375. So vertraulich und heimlich habe ich
icht leicht ein Plätzchen gefunden. G. 14, 14; Wir dachten
s uns so bequem, so artig, so gemütlich und h. 15, 9; In stiller
I—keit, umzielt von engen Schranken. Haller: Einer sorg-
chen Hausfrau, die mit dem Wenigsten eine vergnügliche
I—keit (Häuslichkeit) zu schaffen versteht. Hartmann Unst.
, 188; Desto h—er kam ihm jetzt der ihm erst kurz noch so
remde Mann vor. Kerner 540; Die protestantischen Besitzer
ihlen sich . . . nicht h. unter ihren katholischen Unterthanen.
.ohl. Irl. I, 172; Wenns h. wird und leise/die Abendstille nur
n deiner Zelle lauscht. Tiedge 2, 39; Still und lieb und h., als
e sich/zum Ruhen einen Platz nur wünschen möchten. W. II,
44; Es war ihm garnicht h. dabei 27. 170, etc.—Auch: Der
latz war so still, so einsam, so schatten-h. Scherr Pilg. I, 170;
ie ab- und zuströmenden Fluthwellen, träumend und wiegen-
ed-h. Körner, Sch. 3, 320, etc.—Vgl. namentl. Un-h.—
amentl. bei schwäb., schwzr. Schriftst. oft dreisilbig: Wie
heimelich" war es dann Ivo Abends wieder, als er zu Hause

and security as in one within the four walls of his house.
"Is it still *heimlich* to you in your country where
strangers are felling your woods?" "She did not feel all
too *heimlich* with him." "To destroy the *Heimlichkeit* of
the home." "I could not readily find another spot so
intimate and *heimlich* as this." "In quiet *Heimlichkeit*,
surrounded by close walls." "A careful housewife, who
knows how to make a pleasing *Heimlichkeit* (*Häuslichkeit*)[6] out of the smallest means." "The protestant rulers
do not feel . . . *heimlich* among their catholic subjects."
"When it grows *heimlich* and still, and the evening quiet
alone watches over your cell." "Quiet, lovely and *heimlich*, no place more fitted for her rest." "The in and out-
flowing waves of the current, dreamy and *heimlich* as a
cradle-song." Cf. in especial *Unheimlich*. Among Swa-
bian and Swiss authors in especial, often as trisyllable:
"How *heimelich* it seemed again of an evening, back at
home." "The warm room and the *heimelig* afternoon."
"Little by little they grew at ease and *heimelig* among

---

lag. Auerbach, D. 1, 249; In dem Haus ist mir's so heimelig
gewesen. 4. 307; Die warme Stube, der heimelige Nachmittag
Gotthelf, Sch. 127, 148; Das ist das wahre Heimelig, wenn der
Mensch so von Herzen fühlt, wie wenig er ist, wie gross der
Herr ist. 147; Wurde man nach und nach recht gemütlich und
heimelig mit einander. U. 1, 297; Die trauliche Heimeligkeit
380, 2, 86; Heimelicher wird es mir wohl nirgends werden als
hier. 327; Pestalozzi 4, 240; Was von ferne herkommt . . . lebt
gw. nicht ganz heimelig (heimatlich, freundnachbarlich) mit
den Leuten. 325; Die Hütte, wo/er sonst so heimelig, so froh/
. . . im Kreis der Seinen oft gesessen. Reithard 20; Da klingt
das Horn des Wächters so heimelig vom Thurm/da ladet seine
Stimme so gastlich. 49; Es schläft sich da so lind und warm/so
wunderheim'lig ein. 23, etc.—Diese Weise verdiente allgemein
zu werden, um das gute Wort vor dem Veralten wegen nahe
liegender Verwechslung mit 2 zu bewahren. vgl.: "Die Zecks
sind alle h. (2)" H . . . ? Was verstehen sie unter h . . . ?—
"Nun . . . es kommt mir mit ihnen vor, wie mit einem zugegra-

---

[6] [From *Haus* = house; *Häuslichkeit* = domestic life.—
Trans.]

themselves." "That which comes from afar . . . assuredly does not live quite *heimelig* (*heimatlich* [at home], *freundnachbarlich* [in a neighbourly way]) among the people." "The sentinel's horn sounds so *heimelig* from the tower, and his voice invites so hospitably." *This form of the word ought to become general in order to protect the word from becoming obsolete in its good sense through an easy confusion with II.* [see below]. " 'The Zecks* [a family name] *are all "heimlich."* ' ' *"Heimlich"? What do you understand by "heimlich"?' 'Well, . . . they are like a buried spring or a dried-up pond. One cannot walk over it without always having the feeling that water might come up there again.' 'Oh, we call it "unheimlich"; you call it "heimlich." Well, what makes you think that there is something secret and untrustworthy about this family?' "* Gutzkow.

II. Concealed, kept from sight, so that others do not get to know about it, withheld from others, cf. *geheim* [secret]; so also *Heimlichkeit* for *Geheimnis* [secret].

---

benen Brunnen oder einem ausgetrockneten Teich. Man kann nicht darüber gehen, ohne dass es Einem immer ist, als könnte da wieder einmal Wasser zum Vorschein kommen. Wir nennen das un—h.; Sie nennen's h. Worin finden Sie denn, dass diese Familie etwas Verstecktes und Unzuverlässiges hat? etc. Gutzkow R. 2, 61*).—(*d*) (s. *c*) namentl. schles.: fröhlich, heiter, auch vom Wetter, s. Adelung und Weinhold.—2. versteckt, verborgen gehalten, so dass man Andre nicht davon oder darum wissen lassen, es ihnen verbergen will, vgl. Geheim (2), von welchem erst nhd. Ew. es doch zumal in der älteren Sprache, z. B. in der Bibel, wie Hiob 11, 6; 15, 8, Weish. 2, 22; 1. Kor. 2, 7 etc., und so auch H—keit statt Geheimnis. Math. 13, 35 etc., nicht immer genau geschieden wird: H. (hinter Jemandes Rücken) etwas thun, treiben; Sich h. davon schleichen; H—e Zusammenkünfte, Verabredungen; Mit h—er Schadenfreude zusehen; H. seufzen, weinen; H. thun, als ob man etwas zu verbergen hätte; H—e Liebe, Liebschaft, Sünde; H—e Orte (die der Wohlstand zu verhüllen gebietet), 1. Sam. 5, 6; Das h—e Gemach (Abtritt) 2. Kön. 10, 27; W. 5, 256 etc., auch: Der h—e Stuhl. Zink-

* Sperrdruck (auch im folgenden) vom Referenten.

To do something *heimlich, i.e.* behind someone's back; to steal away *heimlich; heimlich* meetings and appointments; to look on with *heimlich* pleasure at someone's discomfiture; to sigh or weep *heimlich;* to behave *heimlich,* as though there was something to conceal; *heimlich* love, love-affair, sin; *heimlich* places (which good manners oblige us to conceal). 1 Sam, v. 6; "The *heimlich* chamber" [privy]. 2 Kings x. 27 etc.; "To throw into pits or *Heimlichkeit.*" Led the steeds *heimlich* before Laomedon." "As secretive, *heimlich,* deceitful and malicious towards cruel masters . . . as frank, open, sympathetic and helpful towards a friend in misfortune." "The *heimlich* art" (magic). "Where public ventilation has to stop, there *heimlich* machinations begin." "Freedom is the whispered watchword of *heimlich* conspirators and the loud battle-cry of professed revolutionaries." "A holy, *heimlich* effect." "I have roots that are most *heimlich,* I am grown in the deep earth." "My *heimlich* pranks." (Cf. *Heimtücke* [mischief]). To dis-

---

gräf 1, 249; In Graben, in H—keiten werfen. 3, 75; Rollenhagen Fr. 83 etc.—Führte h. vor Laomedon/die Stuten vor. B. 161 b etc.—Ebenso versteckt, h., hinterlistig und boshaft gegen grausame Herren . . . wie offen, frei, theilnehmend und dienstwillig gegen den leidenden Freund. Burmeister g B 2, 157; Du sollst mein h. Heiligstes noch wissen. Chamisso 4, 56; Die h—e Kunst (der Zauberei). 3, 224; Wo die öffentliche Ventilation aufhören muss, fängt die h—e Machination an. Forster, Br. 2, 135; Freiheit ist die leise Parole h. Verschworener, das laute Feldgeschrei der öffentlich Umwälzenden. G. 4, 222; Ein heilig, h. Wirken. 15; Ich habe Wurzeln/die sind gar h.,/im tiefen Boden/bin ich gegründet. 2, 109; Meine h—e Tücke (vgl. Heimtücke). 30, 344; Empfängt er es nicht offenbar und gewissenhaft, so mag er es h. und gewissenlos ergreifen. 39, 22; Liess h. und geheimnisvoll archromatische Fernröhre zusammensetzen. 375; Von nun an, will ich, sei nichts H—es mehr unter uns. Sch. 369 b.—Jemandes H—keiten entdecken, offenbaren, verrathen; H—keiten hinter meinem Rücken zu brauen. Alexis. H. 2, 3, 168; Zu meiner Zeit / befliss man sich der H—keit. Hagedorn 3, 92; Die H—keit und das Gepuschele unter de Hand. Immermann,

cover, disclose, betray someone's *Heimlichkeiten;* "to concoct *Heimlichkeiten* behind my back." Cf. *Geheimnis.*

Compounds and especially also the opposite follow meaning I. (above): *Unheimlich,* uneasy, eerie, blood-curdling; "Seeming almost *unheimlich* and ghostly to him." "I had already long since felt an *unheimlich,* even gruesome feeling." "Feels an *unheimlich* horror." "*Unheimlich* and motionless like a stone-image." "The *unheimlich* mist called hill-fog." "These pale youths are *unheimlich* and are brewing heaven knows what mischief." " '*Unheimlich*' is the name for everything that ought to have remained . . . hidden and secret and has become visible," Schelling. "To veil the divine, to surround it with a certain *Unheimlichkeit.*"—*Unheimlich* is not often used as opposite to meaning II. (above).

What interests us most in this long extract is to find that among its different shades of meaning the word *heim-*

M. 3, 289; Der H—keit (des verborgnen Golds) unmächtigen Bann/kann nur die Hand der Einsicht lösen. Novalis. 1, 69; /Sag an, wo du sie verbirgst . . . in welches Ortes verschwiegener H. Schr. 495 b; Ihr Bienen, die ihr knetet/der H—keiten Schloss (Wachs zum Siegeln). Tieck, Cymb. 3, 2; Erfahren in seltnen H—keiten (Zauberkünsten). Schlegel Sh. 6, 102 etc. vgl. Geheimnis L. 10: 291 ff.

Zsstzg. s. 1 *c,* so auch nam. der Ggstz.: Un-: unbehagliches, banges Grauen erregend: Der schier ihm un-h., gespenstisch erschien. Chamisso 3, 238; Der Nacht un-h. bange Stunden. 4, 148; Mir war schon lang' un-h., ja graulich zu Mute. 242; Nun fängts mir an, un-h. zu werden. Gutzkow R. 2, 82; Empfindet ein u—es Grauen. Verm. 1, 51: Un-h. und starr wie ein Steinbild. Reis, 1, 10; Den u—en Nebel, Haarrauch geheissen. Immermann M., 3, 299; Diese blassen Jungen sind un-h. und brauen Gott weiss was Schlimmes. Laube, Band 1, 119; Un-h. nennt man Alles, was im Geheimnis, im Verborgnen . . . bleiben sollte und hervorgetreten ist. Schelling, 2, 2, 649 etc. —Das Göttliche zu verhüllen, mit einer gewissen U—keit zu umgeben 658, etc.—Unüblich als Ggstz. von (2), wie es Campe ohne Beleg anführt.

lich exhibits one which is identical with its opposite, *un-heimlich*. What is *heimlich* thus comes to be *unheimlich*. (Cf. the quotation from Gutzkow: "We call it *unheimlich*; you call it *heimlich*.") In general we are reminded that the word *heimlich* is not unambiguous, but belongs to two sets of ideas, which without being contradictory are yet very different: on the one hand, it means that which is familiar and congenial, and on the other, that which is concealed and kept out of sight. The word *unheimlich* is only used customarily, we are told, as the contrary of the first signification, and not of the second. Sanders tells us nothing concerning a possible genetic connection between these two sets of meanings. On the other hand, we notice that Schelling says something which throws quite a new light on the concept of the "uncanny," one which we had certainly not awaited. According to him everything is un-canny that ought to have remained hidden and secret, and yet comes to light.

Some of the doubts that have thus arisen are removed if we consult Grimm's dictionary.[7]

[7] Grimm, Jakob und Wilhelm, *Deutsches Wörterbuch,* Leipzig, 1877, IV./2, p. 874 *et seq.*

"Heimlich; adj. und adv. vernaculus, occultus; mhd. heimelîch, heîmlich.

S. 874: In etwas anderem sinne: es ist mir heimlich, wohl, frei von furcht. . . .

(*b*) heimlich ist auch der von gespensterhaften freie ort . . .

S. 875: (ss) vertraut; freundlich, zutraulich.

4. aus dem heimatlichen, häuslichen entwickelt sich weiter der begriff des fremden augen entzogenen, verborgenen, geheimen, eben auch in mehrfacher beziehung ausgebildet . . .

S. 876:   "links am see
        liegt eine matte heimlich im gehölz."
                                Schiller, Tell I., 4.

. . . frei und für den modernen Sprachgebrauch ungewöhnlich . . . heimlich ist zu einem verbum des verbergens gestellt: er verbirgt mich heimlich in seinem gezelt. ps. 27, 5. (. . . heim-liche orte am menschlichen Körper, pudenda . . . welche leute nicht stürben, die wurden geschlagen an heimlichen örten. 1 Samuel 5, 12 . . .

We read.

Heimlich; adj. and adv. *vernaculus, occultus;* MHG. heimelîch, heîmlich.

P. 874. In a slightly different sense: "I feel *heimlich,* well, free from fear. . . ."

(*b*) *Heimlich,* also in the sense of a place free from ghostly influences . . . familiar, friendly, intimate.

4. *From the idea of "homelike," "belonging to the house," the further idea is developed of something withdrawn from the eyes of others, something concealed, secret, and this idea is expanded in many ways.* . . .

P. 876. "On the left bank of the lake there lies a meadow *heimlich* in the wood." Schiller, *Tell.* . . . Poetic licence, rarely so used in modern speech . . . In conjunction with a verb expressing the act of concealing: "In the secret of his tabernacle he shall hide me (*heimlich*)." Ps. xxvii. 5 . . . *Heimlich* places in the human

---

(*c*) Beamtete, die wichtige und geheim zu haltende ratschläge in staatssachen ertheilen, heissen heimliche räthe, das adjektiv nach heutigem sprachgebrauch durch geheim (s.d.) ersetzt: . . . (Pharao) nennet ihn (Joseph) den heimlichen rath. 1. Mos. 41, 45;

S. 878. 6. Heimlich für die erkenntnis, mystisch, allegorisch: heimliche bedeutung, mysticus, divinus, occultus, figuratus.

S. 878. Anders ist heimlich im folgenden, der erkenntnis entzogen, unbewuszt: . . .

Dann aber ist heimlich auch verschlossen, undurchdringlich in bezug auf erforschung: . . .

"Merkst du wohl? sie trauen mir nicht,
fürchten des Friedländers heimlich gesicht."
Wallensteins lager, 2. aufz.

9. die bedeutung des versteckten, gefährlichen, die in der vorigen nummer hervortritt, entwickelt sich noch weiter, so dass heimlich den sinn empfängt, den sonst unheimlich (gebildet nach heimlich, 3*b* sp. 874) hat: "mir ist zu zeiten wie dem menschen der in nacht wandelt und an gespenster glaubt, jeder winkel ist ihm heimlich und schauerhaft." Klinger, theater, 3, 298.

body, pudenda . . . "the men that died not were smitten" (on their *heimlich* parts). 1 Samuel v. 12. . . .

(c) Officials who give important advice which has to be kept secret in matters of state are called *heimlich* councillors; the adjective, according to modern usage, having been replaced by *geheim* [secret]. . . . "Pharaoh called Joseph's name 'him to whom secrets are revealed' " (*heimlich* councillor). Gen. xli. 45.

P. 878. 6. *Heimlich,* as used of knowledge, mystic, allegorical: a *heimlich* meaning, *mysticus, divinus, occultus, figuratus.*

P. 878. *Heimlich* in a different sense, as withdrawn from knowledge, unconscious: . . . *Heimlich* also has the meaning of that which is obscure, inaccessible to knowledge. . . . "Do you not see? They do not trust me; they fear the *heimlich* face of the Duke of Friedland." *Wallensteins Lager,* Act. 2.

9. *The notion of something hidden and dangerous, which is expressed in the last paragraph, is still further developed, so that "heimlich" comes to have the meaning usually ascribed to "unheimlich."* Thus: "At times I feel like a man who walks in the night and believes in ghosts; every corner is *heimlich* and full of terrors for him." Klinger.

Thus *heimlich* is a word the meaning of which develops towards an ambivalence, until it finally coincides with its opposite, *unheimlich. Unheimlich* is in some way or other a sub-species of *heimlich.* Let us retain this discovery, which we do not yet properly understand, alongside of Schelling's definition of the "uncanny." Then if we examine individual instances of uncanniness, these indications will become comprehensible to us.

2

In proceeding to review those things, persons, impressions, events and situations which are able to arouse in us a feeling of the uncanny in a very forcible and definite form, the first requirement is obviously to select a suitable example to start upon. Jentsch has taken as a very good instance "doubts whether an apparently animate being is really alive; or conversely, whether a lifeless object might not be in fact animate"; and he refers in this connection to the impression made by wax-work figures, artificial dolls and automatons. He adds to this class the uncanny effect of epileptic seizures and the manifestations of insanity, because these excite in the spectator the feeling that automatic, mechanical processes are at work, concealed beneath the ordinary appearance of animation. Without entirely accepting the author's view, we will take it as a starting-point for our investigation because it leads us on to consider a writer who has succeeded better than anyone else in producing uncanny effects.

Jentsch says: "In telling a story, one of the most successful devices for easily creating uncanny effects is to leave the reader in uncertainty whether a particular figure in the story is a human being or an automaton; and to do it in such a way that his attention is not directly focused upon his uncertainty, so that he may not be urged to go into the matter and clear it up immediately, since that, as we have said, would quickly dissipate the peculiar emotional effect of the thing. Hoffmann has repeatedly employed this psychological artifice with success in his fantastic narratives."

This observation, undoubtedly a correct one, refers primarily to the story of "The Sand-Man" in Hoffmann's *Nachtstücken*,[8] which contains the original of Olympia, the doll in the first act of Offenbach's opera, *Tales of Hoffmann*. But I cannot think—and I hope that most readers of the story will agree with me—that the theme of the doll, Olympia, who is to all appearances a living being, is by any means the only element to be held responsible for the quite unparalleled atmosphere of uncanniness which the story evokes; or, indeed, that it is the most important among them. Nor is this effect of the story heightened by the fact that the author himself treats

[8] Hoffmann's *Sämtliche Werke*, Grisebach Edition, vol. iii.

the episode of Olympia with a faint touch of satire and uses it to make fun of the young man's idealization of his mistress. The main theme of the story is, on the contrary, something different, something which gives its name to the story, and which is always re-introduced at the critical moment: it is the theme of the "Sand-Man" who tears out children's eyes.

This fantastic tale begins with the childhood-recollections of the student Nathaniel: in spite of his present happiness, he cannot banish the memories associated with the mysterious and terrifying death of the father he loved. On certain evenings his mother used to send the children to bed early, warning them that "the Sand-Man was coming"; and sure enough Nathaniel would not fail to hear the heavy tread of a visitor with whom his father would then be occupied that evening. When questioned about the Sand-Man, his mother, it is true, denied that such a person existed except as a form of speech; but his nurse could give him more definite information: "He is a wicked man who comes when children won't go to bed, and throws handfuls of sand in their eyes so that they jump out of their heads all bleeding. Then he puts the eyes in a sack and carries them off to the moon to feed his children. They sit up there in their nest, and their beaks are hooked like owls' beaks, and they use them to peck up naughty boys' and girls' eyes with."

Although little Nathaniel was sensible and old enough not to believe in such gruesome attributes to the figure of the Sand-Man, yet the dread of him became fixed in his breast. He determined to find out what the Sand-Man looked like; and one evening, when the Sand-Man was again expected, he hid himself in his father's study. He recognized the visitor as the lawyer Coppelius, a repulsive person of whom the children were frightened when he occasionally came to a meal; and he now identified this Coppelius with the dreaded Sand-Man. Concerning the rest of the scene, Hoffmann already leaves us in doubt whether we are witnessing the first delirium of the panic-stricken boy, or a succession of events which are to be regarded in the story as being real. His father and the guest begin to busy themselves at a hearth with glowing flames. The little eavesdropper hears Coppelius call out, "Here with your eyes!" and betrays himself by screaming aloud; Coppelius seizes him and is about to drop grains of red-hot coal out of the fire into his eyes, so as to cast them out on the hearth. His father begs him off and saves his eyes. After this the boy falls into a deep swoon; and a long illness followed upon his experience. Those who lean towards a rationalistic interpretation of the Sand-Man will not fail to recognize in the child's phantasy the continued influence of his nurse's story. The grains of sand that are to be thrown into the child's eyes turn into red-hot grains of coal out of the flames; and in both cases they are meant to make his eyes jump out. In the course of another visit of the Sand-Man's, a year later, his father was killed in his study by an explosion. The lawyer Coppelius vanished from the place without leaving a trace behind.

Nathaniel, now a student, believes that he has recognized this childhood's phantom of horror in an itinerant optician, an Italian called Giuseppe Coppola. This man had offered him barometers for sale in his university town, and when Nathaniel refused had added: "Eh, not barometers, not barometers—also got fine eyes, beautiful eyes." The student's terror was allayed on finding that the proffered eyes were only harmless spectacles, and he bought a pocket-telescope from Coppola. With its aid he looks across into Professor Spalanzani's house opposite and there spies Spalanzani's beautiful, but strangely silent and motionless daughter, Olympia. He soon falls in love with her so violently that he quite forgets his clever and sensible betrothed on her account. But Olympia was an automaton whose works Spalanzani had made, and whose eyes Coppola, the Sand-Man, had put in. The student surprises the two men quarrelling over their handiwork. The optician carries off the wooden eyeless doll; and the mechanician, Spalanzani, takes up Olympia's bleeding eye-balls from the ground and throws them at Nathaniel's breast, saying that Coppola had stolen them from him (Nathaniel). Nathaniel succumbs to a fresh attack of madness, and in his delirium his recollection of his father's death is mingled with this new experience. He cries, "Faster—faster—faster—rings of fire—rings of fire! Whirl about, rings of fire—round and round! Wooden doll, ho! lovely wooden doll, whirl about——," then falls upon the professor, Olympia's so-called father, and tries to strangle him.

Rallying from a long and serious illness, Nathaniel seemed at last to have recovered. He was going to marry his betrothed with whom he was reconciled. One day he was walking through the town and market-place, where the high tower of the Town-Hall threw its huge shadow. On the girl's suggestion they mounted the tower, leaving her brother, who was walking with them, down below. Up there, Clara's attention is drawn to a curious object coming along the street. Nathaniel looks at this thing through Coppola's spy-glass, which he finds in his pocket, and falls into a new fit of madness. Shouting out, "Whirl about, my wooden doll!" he tries to fling the girl into the depths below. Her brother, brought to her side by her cries, rescues her and hastens down to safety with her. Up above, the raving man rushes round, shrieking "Rings of fire, whirl about!"—words whose origin we know. Among the people who begin to gather below there comes forward the figure of the lawyer Coppelius, suddenly returned. We may suppose it was his approach, seen through the telescope, that threw Nathaniel into his madness. People want to go up and overpower the madman, but Coppelius[9] laughs and says, "Wait a bit; he'll come down of himself." Nathaniel suddenly stands still, catches sight of Coppelius, and with a wild shriek "Yes! 'Fine eyes—beautiful eyes,'" flings himself down over the parapet. No sooner does he

[9] Frau Dr. Rank has pointed out the association of the name with "Coppella" = crucible, connecting it with the chemical operations that caused the father's death; and also with "coppo" = eye-socket.

lie on the paving-stones with a shattered skull than the Sand-Man vanishes in the throng.

This short summary leaves, I think, no doubt that the feeling of something uncanny is directly attached to the figure of the Sand-Man, that is, to the idea of being robbed of one's eyes; and that Jentsch's point of an intellectual uncertainty has nothing to do with this effect. Uncertainty whether an object is living or inanimate, which we must admit in regard to the doll Olympia, is quite irrelevant in connection with this other, more striking instance of un-canniness. It is true that the writer creates a kind of un-certainty in us in the beginning by not letting us know, no doubt purposely, whether he is taking us into the real world or into a purely fantastic one of his own creation. He has admitted the right to do either; and if he chooses to stage his action in a world peopled with spirits, demons and ghosts, as Shakespeare does in *Hamlet*, in *Macbeth* and, in a different sense, in *The Tempest* and *A Mid-summer Night's Dream*, we must bow to his decision and treat his setting as though it were real for as long as we put ourselves into his hands. But this uncertainty dis-appears in the course of Hoffmann's story, and we perceive that he means to make us, too, look through the fell Coppola's glasses—perhaps, indeed, that he himself once gazed through such an instrument. For the conclusion of the story makes it quite clear that Coppola the optician really is the lawyer Coppelius and thus also the Sand-Man.

There is no question, therefore, of any "intellectual uncertainty"; we know now that we are not supposed to be looking on at the products of a madman's imagination behind which we, with the superiority of rational minds, are able to detect the sober truth; and yet this knowledge does not lessen the impression of uncanniness in the least degree. The theory of "intellectual uncertainty" is thus incapable of explaining that impression.

We know from psychoanalytic experience, however, that this fear of damaging or losing one's eyes is a terrible fear of childhood. Many adults still retain their apprehensiveness in this respect, and no bodily injury is so much dreaded by them as an injury to the eye. We are accustomed to say, too, that we will treasure a thing as the apple of our eye. A study of dreams, phantasies and myths has taught us that a morbid anxiety connected with the eyes and with going blind is often enough a substitute for the dread of castration. In blinding himself, Oedipus, that mythical law-breaker, was simply carrying out a mitigated form of the punishment of castration—the only punishment that according to the *lex talionis* was fitted for him. We may try to reject the derivation of fears about the eye from the fear of castration on rationalistic grounds, and say that it is very natural that so precious an organ as the eye should be guarded by a proportionate dread; indeed, we might go further and say that the fear of castration itself contains no other significance and no deeper secret than a justifiable dread of this kind. But this view does not account adequately for the substitutive relation between the eye and the male member which is seen to exist in dreams and myths and phantasies; nor can it dispel the impression one gains that it is the threat of being castrated in especial which excites a peculiarly violent and obscure emotion, and that this emotion is what first gives the idea of losing other organs its intense colouring. All further doubts are removed when we get the details of their "castration-complex" from the analyses of neurotic patients, and realize its immense importance in their mental life.

Moreover, I would not recommend any opponent of the psychoanalytic view to select precisely the story of the Sand-Man upon which to build his case that morbid anxiety about the eyes has nothing to do with the castration-complex. For why does Hoffmann bring the anxiety about eyes into such intimate connection with the father's death? And why does the Sand-Man appear each time in order to interfere with love? He divides the unfortunate Nathaniel from his betrothed and from her brother, his best friend; he destroys his second object of love, Olympia, the lovely doll; and he drives him into suicide at the moment when he has won back his Clara and is about to be happily united to her. Things like these and many more seem arbitrary and meaningless in the story so long as we deny all connection between fears about the eye and castration; but they become intelligible as soon as we replace the Sand-Man by the dreaded father at whose hands castration is awaited.[10]

We shall venture, therefore, to refer the uncanny effect of the Sand-Man to the child's dread in relation to its castration-complex. But having gained the idea that we can take this infantile factor to account for feelings of uncanniness, we are drawn to examine whether we can apply it to other instances of uncanny things. We find in the story of the Sand-Man the other theme upon which Jentsch lays stress, of a doll that appears to be alive. Jentsch believes that a particularly favourable condition for awakening uncanny sensations is created when there is intellectual uncertainty whether an object is alive or not, and when an inanimate object becomes too much like an animate one. Now, dolls happen to be rather closely connected with infantile life. We remember that in their early games children do not distinguish at all sharply

[10] In fact, Hoffmann's imaginative treatment of his material has not played such havoc with its elements that we cannot reconstruct their original arrangement. In the story from Nathaniel's childhood, the figures of his father and Coppelius represent the two opposites into which the father-imago is split by the ambivalence of the child's feeling; whereas the one threatens to blind him, that is, to castrate him, the other, the loving father, intercedes for his sight. That part of the complex which is most strongly repressed, the death-wish against the father, finds expression in the death of the good father, and Coppelius is made answerable for it. Later, in his student days, Professor Spalanzani and Coppola the optician reproduce this double representation of the father-imago, the Professor as a member of the father-series, Coppola openly identified with the lawyer Coppelius. Just as before they used to work together over the fire, so now they have jointly created the doll Olympia; the Professor is even called the father of Olympia. This second occurrence of work in common shows

between living and lifeless objects, and that they are especially fond of treating their dolls like live people. In fact I have occasionally heard a woman patient declare that even at the age of eight she had still been convinced that her dolls would be certain to come to life if she were to look at them in a particular way, with as concentrated a gaze as possible. So that here, too, it is not difficult to discover a factor from childhood; but curiously enough, while the Sand-Man story deals with the excitation of an early childhood fear, the idea of a "living doll" excites no fear at all; the child had no fear of its doll coming to life, it may even have desired it. The source of the feeling of an uncanny thing would not, therefore, be an infantile fear in this case, but rather an infantile wish or even only an infantile belief. There seems to be a contradiction here; but perhaps it is only a complication, which may be helpful to us later on.

Hoffmann is in literature the unrivalled master of conjuring up the uncanny. His *Elixire des Teufels* [The Devil's Elixir] contains a mass of themes to which one is tempted to ascribe the uncanny effect of the narrative; but it is too obscure and intricate a story to venture to summarize. Towards the end of the book the reader is told the facts,

---

that the optician and the mechanician are also components of the father-imago, that is, both are Nathaniel's father as well as Olympia's. I ought to have added that in the terrifying scene in childhood, Coppelius, after sparing Nathaniel's eyes, had screwed off his arms and legs as an experiment; that is, he had experimented on him as a mechanician would on a doll. This singular feature, which seems quite out of perspective in the picture of the Sand-Man, introduces a new castration-equivalent; but it also emphasizes the identity of Coppelius and his later counterpart, Spalanzani the mechanician, and helps us to understand who Olympia is. She, the automatic doll, can be nothing else than a personification of Nathaniel's feminine attitude towards his father in his infancy. The father of both, Spalanzani and Coppola, are, as we know, new editions, reincarnations of Nathaniel's "two" fathers. Now Spalanzani's otherwise incomprehensible statement that the optician has

hitherto concealed from him, from which the action springs; with the result, not that he is at last enlightened, but that he falls into a state of complete bewilderment. The author has piled up too much of a kind; one's comprehension of the whole suffers as a result, though not the impression it makes. We must content ourselves with selecting those themes of uncanniness which are most prominent, and seeing whether we can fairly trace them also back to infantile sources. These themes are all concerned with the idea of a "double" in every shape and degree, with persons, therefore, who are to be considered identical by reason of looking alike; Hoffmann accentuates this relation by transferring mental processes from the one person to the other—what we should call telepathy—so that the one possesses knowledge, feeling and experience in common with the other, identifies himself with another person, so that his self becomes confounded, or the foreign self is substituted for his own—in other words, by doubling, dividing and interchanging the self. And finally there is the constant recurrence of similar situations, a same face, or character-trait, or twist of fortune, or a same

---

stolen Nathaniel's eyes so as to set them in the doll becomes significant and supplies fresh evidence for the identity of Olympia and Nathaniel. Olympia is, as it were, a dissociated complex of Nathaniel's which confronts him as a person, and Nathaniel's enslavement to this complex is expressed in his senseless obsessive love for Olympia. We may with justice call such love narcissistic, and can understand why he who has fallen victim to it should relinquish his real, external object of love. The psychological truth of the situation in which the young man, fixated upon his father by his castration-complex, is incapable of loving a woman, is amply proved by numerous analyses of patients whose story, though less fantastic, is hardly less tragic than that of the student Nathaniel.

Hoffmann was the child of an unhappy marriage. When he was three years old, his father left his small family, never to be united to them again. According to Grisebach, in his biographical introduction to Hoffmann's works, the writer's relation to his father was always a most sensitive subject with him.

crime, or even a same name recurring throughout several consecutive generations.

The theme of the "double" has been very thoroughly treated by Otto Rank.[11] He has gone into the connections the "double" has with reflections in mirrors, with shadows, guardian spirits, with the belief in the soul and the fear of death; but he also lets in a flood of light on the astonishing evolution of this idea. For the "double" was originally an insurance against destruction to the ego, an "energetic denial of the power of death," as Rank says; and probably the "immortal" soul was the first "double" of the body. This invention of doubling as a preservation against extinction has its counterpart in the language of dreams, which is fond of representing castration by a doubling or multiplication of the genital symbol; the same desire spurred on the ancient Egyptians to the art of making images of the dead in some lasting material. Such ideas, however, have sprung from the soil of unbounded self-love, from the primary narcissism which holds sway in the mind of the child as in that of primitive man; and when this stage has been left behind the double takes on a different aspect. From having been an assurance of immortality, he becomes the ghastly harbinger of death.

The idea of the "double" does not necessarily disappear with the passing of the primary narcissism, for it can receive fresh meaning from the later stages of development of the ego. A special faculty is slowly formed there, able to oppose the rest of the ego, with the function of observing and criticizing the self and exercising a censorship within the mind, and this we become aware of as our "conscience." In the pathological case of delusions of being watched this mental institution becomes isolated, dissociated from the ego, and discernible to a physician's eye. The fact that a faculty of this kind exists, which is able to treat the rest of the ego like an object—the fact, that is, that man is capable of self-observation—renders it possible to invest the old idea of a "double" with a new meaning

[11] "Der Doppelgänger."

and to ascribe many things to it, above all, those things which seem to the new faculty of self-criticism to belong to the old surmounted narcissism of the earliest period of all.[12]

But it is not only this narcissism, offensive to the ego-criticizing faculty, which may be incorporated in the idea of a double. There are also all those unfulfilled but possible futures to which we still like to cling in phantasy, all those strivings of the ego which adverse external circumstances have crushed, and all our suppressed acts of volition which nourish in us the illusion of Free Will.[13]

But, after having thus considered the manifest motivation of the figure of a "double," we have to admit that none of it helps us to understand the extraordinarily strong feeling of something uncanny that pervades the conception; and our knowledge of pathological mental processes enables us to add that nothing in the content arrived at could account for that impulse towards self-protection which has caused the ego to project such a content outward as something foreign to itself. The quality of uncanniness can only come from the circumstance of the "double" being a creation dating back to a very early mental stage, long since left behind, and one, no doubt, in which it wore a more friendly aspect. The "double" has become a vision

---

[12] I cannot help thinking that when poets complain that two souls dwell within the human breast, and when popular psychologists talk of the splitting of the ego in an individual, they have some notion of this division (which relates to the sphere of ego-psychology) between the critical faculty and the rest of the ego, and not of the antithesis discovered by psychoanalysis between the ego and what is unconscious and repressed. It is true that the distinction is to some extent effaced by the circumstance that derivatives of what is repressed are foremost among the things reprehended by the ego-criticizing faculty.

[13] In Ewers' *Der Student von Prag,* which furnishes the starting-point of Rank's study on the "double," the hero has promised his beloved not to kill his antagonist in a duel. But on his way to the duelling-ground he meets his "double," who has already killed his rival.

of terror, just as after the fall of their religion the gods took on daemonic shapes.[14]

It is not difficult to judge, on the same lines as his theme of the "double," the other forms of disturbance in the ego made use of by Hoffmann. They are a harking-back to particular phases in the evolution of the self-regarding feeling, a regression to a time when the ego was not yet sharply differentiated from the external world and from other persons. I believe that these factors are partly responsible for the impression of the uncanny, although it is not easy to isolate and determine exactly their share of it.

That factor which consists in a recurrence of the same situations, things and events, will perhaps not appeal to everyone as a source of uncanny feeling. From what I have observed, this phenomenon does undoubtedly, subject to certain conditions and combined with certain circumstances, awaken an uncanny feeling, which recalls that sense of helplessness sometimes experienced in dreams. Once, as I was walking through the deserted streets of a provincial town in Italy which was strange to me, on a hot summer afternoon, I found myself in a quarter the character of which could not long remain in doubt. Nothing but painted women were to be seen at the windows of the small houses, and I hastened to leave the narrow street at the next turning. But after having wandered about for a while without being directed, I suddenly found myself back in the same street, where my presence was now beginning to excite attention. I hurried away once more, but only to arrive yet a third time by devious paths in the same place. Now, however, a feeling overcame me which I can only describe as uncanny, and I was glad enough to abandon my exploratory walk and get straight back to the piazza I had left a short while before. Other situations having in common with my adventure an involuntary return to the same situation, but which differ radically from it in other respects, also result in the same feeling

[14] Heine, *Die Götter im Exil.*

of helplessness and of something uncanny. As, for instance, when one is lost in a forest in high altitudes, caught, we will suppose, by the mountain mist, and when every endeavor to find the marked or familiar path ends again and again in a return to one and the same spot, recognizable by some particular landmark. Or when one wanders about in a dark, strange room, looking for the door or the electric switch, and collides for the hundredth time with the same piece of furniture—a situation which, indeed, has been made irresistibly comic by Mark Twain, through the wild extravagance of his narration.

Taking another class of things, it is easy to see that here, too, it is only this factor of involuntary repetition which surrounds with an uncanny atmosphere what would otherwise be innocent enough, and forces upon us the idea of something fateful and unescapable where otherwise we should have spoken of "chance" only. For instance, we of course attach no importance to the event when we give up a coat and get a cloakroom ticket with the number, say, 62; or when we find that our cabin on board ship is numbered 62. But the impression is altered if two such events, each in itself indifferent, happen close together, if we come across the number 62 several times in a single day, or if we begin to notice that everything which has a number—addresses, hotel-rooms, compartments in railway-trains—always has the same one, or one which at least contains the same figures. We do feel this to be "uncanny," and unless a man is utterly hardened and proof against the lure of superstition he will be tempted to ascribe a secret meaning to this obstinate recurrence of a number, taking it, perhaps, as an indication of the span of life allotted to him. Or take the case that one is engaged at the time in reading the works of Hering, the famous physiologist, and then receives within the space of a few days two letters from two different countries, each from a person called Hering; whereas one has never before had any dealings with anyone of that name. Not long ago an ingenious scientist attempted to reduce coincidences of this kind to certain laws, and so deprive them of their uncanny effect.[15] I will not venture to decide whether he has succeeded or not.

How exactly we can trace back the uncanny effect of such recurrent similarities to infantile psychology is a question I can only lightly touch upon in these pages; and I must refer the reader instead to another pamphlet,[16] now ready for publication, in which this has been gone into in detail, but in a different connection. It must be explained that we are able to postulate the principle of a *repetition-compulsion* in the unconscious mind, based upon instinctual activity and probably inherent in the very nature of the instincts—a principle powerful enough to overrule the pleasure-principle, lending to certain aspects of the mind their daemonic character, and still very clearly expressed in the tendencies of small children; a principle, too, which is responsible for a part of the course taken by the analyses of neurotic patients. Taken in all, the foregoing prepares us for the discovery that whatever reminds us of this inner *repetition-compulsion* is perceived as uncanny.

Now, however, it is time to turn from these aspects of the matter, which are in any case difficult to decide upon, and look for undeniable instances of the uncanny, in the hope that analysis of them will settle whether our hypothesis is a valid one.

In the story of "The Ring of Polycrates," the guest turns away from his friend with horror because he sees that his every wish is at once fulfilled, his every care immediately removed by kindly fate. His host has become "uncanny" to him. His own explanation, that the too fortunate man has to fear the envy of the gods, seems still rather obscure to us; its meaning is veiled in mythological language. We will therefore turn to another example in a less grandiose setting. In the case history of an obsessional neurotic,[17] I have described how the patient once stayed in a hydropathic establishment and benefited greatly by it. He had

[15] P. Kammerer, *Das Gesetz der Serie* (Vienna, 1919).

[16] [*Beyond the Pleasure-Principle.*—Trans.]

[17] Freud, "Notes upon a Case of Obsessional Neurosis," *Three Case Histories,* Collier Books edition BS 191V.

the good sense, however, to attribute his improvement not to the therapeutic properties of the water, but to the situation of his room, which immediately adjoined that of a very amiable nurse. So on his second visit to the establishment he asked for the same room but was told that it was already occupied by an old gentleman, whereupon he gave vent to his annoyance in the words "Well, I hope he'll have a stroke and die." A fortnight later the old gentleman really did have a stroke. My patient thought this an "uncanny" experience. And that impression of uncanniness would have been stronger still if less time had elapsed between his exclamation and the untoward event, or if he had been able to produce innumerable similar coincidences. As a matter of fact, he had no difficulty in producing coincidences of this sort, but then not only he but all obsessional neurotics I have observed are able to relate analogous experiences. They are never surprised when they invariably run up against the person they have just been thinking of, perhaps for the first time for many months. If they say one day "I haven't had news of so-and-so for a long time," they will be sure to get a letter from him the next morning. And an accident or a death will rarely take place without having cast its shadow before on their minds. They are in the habit of mentioning this state of affairs in the most modest manner, saying that they have "presentiments" which "usually" come true.

One of the most uncanny and wide-spread forms of superstition is the dread of the evil eye.[18] There never seems to have been any doubt about the source of this dread. Whoever possesses something at once valuable and fragile is afraid of the envy of others, in that he projects on to them the envy he would have felt in their place. A feeling like this betrays itself in a look even though it is not put into words; and when a man attracts the attention of others by noticeable, and particularly by unattractive,

[18] Seligmann, the Hamburg ophthalmologist, has made a thorough study of this superstition in his *Der böse Blick und Verwandtes* (Berlin, 1910).

attributes, they are ready to believe that his envy is rising to more than usual heights and that this intensity in it will convert it into effective action. What is feared is thus a secret intention of harming someone, and certain signs are taken to mean that such an intention is capable of becoming an act.

These last examples of the uncanny are to be referred to that principle in the mind which I have called "omnipotence of thoughts," taking the name from an expression used by one of my patients. And now we find ourselves on well-known ground. Our analysis of instances of the uncanny has led us back to the old, animistic conception of the universe, which was characterized by the idea that the world was peopled with the spirits of human beings, and by the narcissistic overestimation of subjective mental processes (such as the belief in the omnipotence of thoughts, the magical practices based upon this belief, the carefully proportioned distribution of magical powers or "mana" among various outside persons and things), as well as by all those other figments of the imagination with which man, in the unrestricted narcissism of that stage of development, strove to withstand the inexorable laws of reality. It would seem as though each one of us has been through a phase of individual development corresponding to that animistic stage in primitive men, that none of us has traversed it without preserving certain traces of it which can be re-activated, and that everything which now strikes us as "uncanny" fulfils the condition of stirring those vestiges of animistic mental activity within us and bringing them to expression.[19]

This is the place now to put forward two considerations which, I think, contain the gist of this short study. In

---

[19] Cf. my book *Totem und Tabu*, part iii., "Animismus, Magie und Allmacht der Gedanken"; also the footnote on p. 7 of the same book: "It would appear that we invest with a feeling of uncanniness those impressions which lend support to a belief in the omnipotence of thoughts, and to the animistic attitude of mind, at a time when our judgment has already rejected these same beliefs."

the first place, if psychoanalytic theory is correct in maintaining that every emotional affect, whatever its quality, is transformed by repression into morbid anxiety, then among such cases of anxiety there must be a class in which the anxiety can be shown to come from something repressed which *recurs*. This class of morbid anxiety would then be no other than what is uncanny, irrespective of whether it originally aroused dread or some other affect. In the second place, if this is indeed the secret nature of the uncanny, we can understand why the usage of speech has extended *das Heimliche* into its opposite *das Unheimliche;* [20] for this uncanny is in reality nothing new or foreign, but something familiar and old-established in the mind that has been estranged only by the process of repression. This reference to the factor of repression enables us, furthermore, to understand Schelling's definition of the uncanny as something which ought to have been kept concealed but which has nevertheless come to light.

It only remains for us to test our new hypothesis on one or two more examples of the uncanny.

Many people experience the feeling in the highest degree in relation to death and dead bodies, to the return of the dead, and to spirits and ghosts. As we have seen, many languages in use to-day can only render the German expression "an *unheimliches* house" by "a *haunted* house." We might indeed have begun our investigation with this example, perhaps the most striking of all, of something uncanny, but we refrained from doing so because the uncanny in it is too much mingled with and in part covered by what is purely gruesome. There is scarcely any other matter, however, upon which our thoughts and feelings have changed so little since the very earliest times, and in which discarded forms have been so completely preserved under a thin disguise, as that of our relation to death. Two things account for our conservatism: the strength of our original emotional reaction to it, and the insufficiency of our scientific knowledge about it. Biology has not yet been

[29] Cf. abstract on p. 23.

able to decide whether death is the inevitable fate of every living being or whether it is only a regular but yet perhaps avoidable event in life. It is true that the proposition "All men are mortal" is paraded in text-books of logic as an example of a generalization, but no human being really grasps it, and our unconscious has as little use now as ever for the idea of its own mortality. Religions continue to dispute the undeniable fact of the death of each one of us and to postulate a life after death; civil governments still believe that they cannot maintain moral order among the living if they do not uphold this prospect of a better life after death as a recompense for earthly existence. In our great cities, placards announce lectures which will tell us how to get into touch with the souls of the departed; and it cannot be denied that many of the most able and penetrating minds among our scientific men have come to the conclusion, especially towards the close of their lives, that a contact of this kind is not utterly impossible. Since practically all of us still think as savages do on this topic, it is no matter for surprise that the primitive fear of the dead is still so strong within us and always ready to come to the surface at any opportunity. Most likely our fear still contains the old belief that the deceased becomes the enemy of his survivor and wants to carry him off to share his new life with him. Considering our unchanged attitude towards death, we might rather inquire what has become of the repression, that necessary condition for enabling a primitive feeling to recur in the shape of an uncanny effect. But repression is there, too. All so-called educated people have ceased to believe, officially at any rate, that the dead can become visible as spirits, and have hedged round any such appearances with improbable and remote circumstances; their emotional attitude towards their dead, moreover, once a highly dubious and ambivalent one, has been toned down in the higher strata of the mind into a simple feeling of reverence.[21]

We have now only a few more remarks to add, for

---

[21] Cf. *Totem und Tabu:* "Das Tabu und die Ambivalenz."

animism, magic and witchcraft, the omnipotence of thoughts, man's attitude to death, involuntary repetition and the castration-complex comprise practically all the factors which turn something fearful into an uncanny thing.

We also call a living person uncanny, usually when we ascribe evil motives to him. But that is not all; we must not only credit him with bad intentions but must attribute to these intentions capacity to achieve their aim in virtue of certain special powers. A good instance of this is the "Gettatore," that uncanny figure of Roman superstitution which Schaeffer, with intuitive poetic feeling and profound psychoanalytic knowledge, has transformed into a sympathetic figure in his *Josef Montfort*. But the question of these secret powers brings us back again to the realm of animism. It is her intuition that he possesses secret power of this kind that makes Mephistopheles so uncanny to the pious Gretchen. "She divines that I am certainly a spirit, even the devil himself perchance."[22]

The uncanny effect of epilepsy and of madness has the same origin. The ordinary person sees in them the workings of forces hitherto unsuspected in his fellow-man but which at the same time he is dimly aware of in a remote corner of his own being. The Middle Ages quite consistently ascribed all such maladies to daemonic influences, and in this their psychology was not so far out. Indeed, I should not be surprised to hear that psychoanalysis, which is concerned with laying bare these hidden forces, has itself become uncanny to many people for that very reason. In one case, after I had succeeded—though none too rapidly—in effecting a cure which had lasted many years in a girl who had been an invalid, the patient's own mother confessed to this attitude long after the girl's recovery.

Dismembered limbs, a severed head, a hand cut off at the wrist,[23] feet which dance by themselves[24]—all these

22   "Sie ahnt, dass ich ganz sicher ein Genie,
          Vielleicht sogar der Teufel bin."
23 Cf. a fairy-tale of Hauff's.
24 As in Schaeffer's book mentioned above.

have something peculiarly uncanny about them, especially when, as in the last instance, they prove able to move of themselves in addition. As we already know, this kind of uncanniness springs from its association with the castration-complex. To many people the idea of being buried alive while appearing to be dead is the most uncanny thing of all. And yet psychoanalysis has taught us that this terrifying phantasy is only a transformation of another phantasy which had originally nothing terrifying about it at all, but was filled with a certain lustful pleasure—the phantasy, I mean, of intra-uterine existence.

There is one more point of general application I should like to add, though, strictly speaking, it has been included in our statements about animism and mechanisms in the mind that have been surmounted; for I think it deserves special mention. This is that an uncanny effect is often and easily produced by effacing the distinction between imagination and reality, such as when something that we have hitherto regarded as imaginary appears before us in reality, or when a symbol takes over the full functions and significance of the thing it symbolizes, and so on. It is this element which contributes not a little to the uncanny effect attaching to magical practices. The infantile element in this, which also holds sway in the minds of neurotics, is the over-accentuation of psychical reality in comparison with physical reality—a feature closely allied to the belief in the omnipotence of thoughts. In the midst of the isolation of war-time a number of the English *Strand Magazine* fell into my hands; and, amongst other not very interesting matter, I read a story about a young married couple, who move into a furnished flat in which there is a curiously shaped table with carvings of crocodiles on it. Towards evening they begin to smell an intolerable and very typical odour that pervades the whole flat; things begin to get in their way and trip them up in the darkness; they seem to see a vague form gliding up the stairs—in short, we are given to understand that the presence of the table causes ghostly crocodiles to haunt the place, or that the wooden monsters come to life in the dark, or something of that sort. It was a thoroughly silly story, but the uncanny feeling it produced was quite remarkable.

To conclude this collection of examples, which is certainly not complete, I will relate an instance taken from psychoanalytical experience; if it does not rest upon mere coincidence, it furnishes a beautiful confirmation of our theory of the uncanny. It often happens that male patients declare that they feel there is something uncanny about the female genital organs. This *unheimlich* place, however, is the entrance to the former *heim* [home] of all human beings, to the place where everyone dwelt once upon a time and in the beginning. There is a humorous saying: "Love is home-sickness"; and whenever a man dreams of a place or a country and says to himself, still in the dream, "this place is familiar to me, I have been there before," we may interpret the place as being his mother's genitals or her body. In this case, too, the *unheimlich* is what was once *heimisch,* home-like, familiar; the prefix "un" is the token of repression.

3

Having followed the discussion as far as this the reader will have felt certain doubts arising in his mind about much that has been said; and he must now have an opportunity of collecting them and bringing them forward.

It may be true that the uncanny is nothing else than a hidden, familiar thing that has undergone repression and then emerged from it, and that everything that is uncanny fulfils this condition. But these factors do not solve the problem of the uncanny. For our proposition is clearly not convertible. Not everything that fulfils this condition—not everything that is connected with repressed desires and archaic forms of thought belonging to the past of the individual and of the race—is therefore uncanny.

Nor would we, moreover, conceal the fact that for almost every example adduced in support of our hypothesis some other analogous one may be found which rebuts it. The story of the severed hand in Hauff's fairy-tale certainly has an uncanny effect, and we have derived that effect from the castration-complex. But in the story in Herodotus of the treasure of Rhampsenitus, where the master-thief leaves his brother's severed hand behind him in that of the princess who wants to hold him fast, most readers will agree with me that the episode has no trace of uncanniness. Again, the instant fulfilment of the king's wishes in "The Ring of Polycrates" undoubtedly does affect us in the same uncanny way as it did the king of Egypt. Yet our own fairy-tales are crammed with instantaneous wish-fulfilments which produce no uncanny effect whatever. In the story of "The Three Wishes," the woman is tempted by the savoury smell of a sausage to wish that she might have one too, and immediately it lies on a plate before her. In his annoyance at her forwardness her husband wishes it may hang on her nose. And there it is, dangling from her nose. All this is very vivid but not in the least uncanny. Fairy-tales quite frankly adopt the animistic standpoint of the omnipotence of thoughts and wishes, and yet I cannot think of any genuine fairy-story which has anything uncanny about it. We have heard that it is in the highest degree uncanny when inanimate objects —a picture or a doll—come to life; nevertheless in Hans Andersen's stories the household utensils, furniture and tin soldiers are alive and nothing could perhaps be more remote from the uncanny. And we should hardly call it uncanny when Pygmalion's beautiful statue comes to life.

Catalepsy and the re-animation of the dead have been represented as most uncanny themes. But things of this sort again are very common in fairy-stories. Who would be so bold as to call it an uncanny moment, for instance, when Snow-White opens her eyes once more? And the resuscitation of the dead in miracles, as in the New Testament, elicits feelings quite unrelated to the uncanny. Then the theme that achieves such an indubitably uncanny effect, the involuntary recurrence of the like, serves, too, other and quite different purposes in another class of cases. One case we have already heard about in which it is employed to call forth a feeling of the comic; and we could multiply instances of this kind. Or again, it works as a means of emphasis, and so on. Another consideration is this: whence come the uncanny influences of silence, darkness and solitude? Do not these factors point to the part played by danger in the aetiology of what is uncanny, notwithstanding that they are also the most frequent accompaniment of the expression of fear in infancy? And are we in truth justified in entirely ignoring intellectual uncertainty as a factor, seeing that we have admitted its importance in relation to death?

It is evident that we must be prepared to admit that there are other elements besides those set down here determining the production of uncanny feelings. We might say that these preliminary results have satisfied psychoanalytic interest in the problem of the uncanny, and that what remains probably calls for an aesthetic valuation. But that would be to open the door to doubts about the exact value of our general contention that the uncanny proceeds from something familiar which has been repressed.

One thing we may observe which may help us to resolve these uncertainties: nearly all the instances which contradict our hypothesis are taken from the realm of fiction and literary productions. This may suggest a possible differentiation between the uncanny that is actually experienced, and the uncanny as we merely picture it or read about it.

Something uncanny in *real experience* is conditioned much more simply, but is limited to much fewer occasions. We shall find, I think, that it fits in perfectly with our attempt at solution, and can be traced back without exception to something familiar that has been repressed. But here, too, we must make a certain important and psychologically significant differentiation in our material, best illustrated by turning to suitable examples.

Let us take the uncanny in connection with the omnipotence of thoughts, instantaneous wish-fulfilments, secret power to do harm and the return of the dead. The condition under which the feeling of uncanniness arises here is unmistakable. We—or our primitive forefathers—once believed in the possibility of these things and were convinced that they really happened. Nowadays we no longer believe in them, we have *surmounted* such ways of thought; but we do not feel quite sure of our new set of beliefs, and the old ones still exist within us ready to seize upon any confirmation. As soon as something actually happens in our lives which seems to support the old, discarded beliefs, we get a feeling of the uncanny; and it is as though we were making a judgement something like this: "So, after all, it is true that one can kill a person by merely desiring his death!" or, "Then the dead do continue to live and appear before our eyes on the scene of their former activities!", and so on. And conversely, he who has completely and finally dispelled animistic beliefs in himself, will be insensible to this type of the uncanny. The most remarkable coincidences of desire and fulfilment, the most mysterious recurrence of similar experiences in a particular place or on a particular date, the most deceptive sights and suspicious noises—none of these things will take him in or raise that kind of fear which can be described as "a fear of something uncanny." For the whole matter is one of "testing reality," pure and simple, a question of the material reality of the phenomena.[25]

The state of affairs is somewhat different when the uncanny proceeds from repressed infantile complexes, from the castration-complex, womb-phantasies, etc.; but experi-

[25] Since the uncanny effect of a "double" also belongs to this class, it is interesting to observe what the effect is of suddenly and unexpectedly meeting one's own image. E. Mach has related two such observations in his *Analyse der Empfindungen* (1900, p. 3). On the first occasion he started violently as soon as he realized that the face before him was his own. The second time he formed a very unfavourable opinion about the supposed stranger who got into the omnibus, and thought

ences which arouse this kind of uncanny feeling are not of very frequent occurrence in real life. Actual occurrences of the uncanny belong for the most part to the first group; nevertheless the distinction between the two is theoretically very important. Where the uncanny comes from infantile complexes the question of external reality is quite irrelevant; its place is taken by psychical reality. What is concerned is an actual repression of some definite material and a return of this repressed material, not a removal of the *belief* in its objective reality. We might say that in the one case what had been repressed was a particular ideational content and in the other the belief in its physical existence. But this last way of putting it no doubt strains the term "repression" beyond its legitimate meaning. It would be more correct to respect a perceptible psychological difference here, and to say that the animistic beliefs of civilized people have been *surmounted*—more or less. Our conclusion could then be stated thus: An uncanny experience occurs either when repressed infantile complexes have been revived by some impression, or when the primitive beliefs we have surmounted seem once more to be confirmed. Finally, we must not let our predilection for smooth solution and lucid exposition blind us to the fact that these two classes of uncanny experience are not always sharply distinguishable. When we consider that primitive beliefs are most intimately connected with infantile complexes, and are, in fact, based upon them, we shall not be greatly astonished to find the distinction often rather a hazy one.

"What a shabby-looking school-master that is getting in now."
—I can supply a similar experience. I was sitting alone in my *wagon-lit* compartment when a more than usually violent jerk of the train swung back the door of the adjoining washing-cabinet, and an elderly gentleman in a dressing-gown and a travelling cap came in. I assumed that he had been about to leave the washing-cabinet which divides the two compartments, and had taken the wrong direction and come into my

The uncanny as it is depicted in *literature,* in stories and imaginative productions, merits in truth a separate discussion. To begin with, it is a much more fertile province than the uncanny in real life, for it contains the whole of the latter and something more besides, something that cannot be found in real life. The distinction between what has been repressed and what has been surmounted cannot be transposed on to the uncanny in fiction without profound modification; for the realm of phantasy depends for its very existence on the fact that its content is not submitted to the reality-testing faculty. The somewhat paradoxical result is that *in the first place a great deal that is not uncanny in fiction would be so if it happened in real life; and in the second place that there are many more means of creating uncanny effects in fiction than there are in real life.*

The story-teller has this licence among many others, that he can select his world of representation so that it either coincides with the realities we are familiar with or departs from them in what particulars he pleases. We accept his ruling in every case. In fairy-tales, for instance, the world of reality is left behind from the very start, and the animistic system of beliefs is frankly adopted. Wish-fulfilments, secret powers, omnipotence of thoughts, animation of lifeless objects, all the elements so common in fairy-stories, can exert no uncanny influence here; for, as we have learnt, that feeling cannot arise unless there is a conflict of judgement whether things which have been

---

compartment by mistake. Jumping up with the intention of putting him right, I at once realized to my dismay that the intruder was nothing but my own reflection in the looking-glass of the open door. I can still recollect that I thoroughly disliked his appearance. Instead, therefore, of being terrified by our doubles, both Mach and I simply failed to recognize them as such. Is it not possible, though, that our dislike of them was a vestigial trace of that older reaction which feels the double to be something uncanny?

"surmounted" and are regarded as incredible are not, after all, possible; and this problem is excluded from the beginning by the setting of the story. And thus we see that such stories as have furnished us with most of the contradictions to our hypothesis of the uncanny confirm the first part of our proposition—that in the realm of fiction many things are not uncanny which would be so if they happened in real life. In the case of the fairy-story there are other contributory factors, which we shall briefly touch upon later.

The story-teller can also choose a setting which, though less imaginary than the world of fairy tales, does yet differ from the real world by admitting superior spiritual entities such as daemonic influences or departed spirits. So long as they remain within their setting of poetic reality their usual attribute of uncanniness fails to attach to such beings. The souls in Dante's *Inferno*, or the ghostly apparitions in *Hamlet, Macbeth* or *Julius Caesar,* may be gloomy and terrible enough, but they are no more really uncanny than is Homer's jovial world of gods. We order our judgement to the imaginary reality imposed on us by the writer, and regard souls, spirits and spectres as though their existence had the same validity in their world as our own has in the external world. And then in this case too we are spared all trace of the uncanny.

The situation is altered as soon as the writer pretends to move in the world of common reality. In this case he accepts all the conditions operating to produce uncanny feelings in real life; and everything that would have an uncanny effect in reality has it in his story. But in this case, too, he can increase his effect and multiply it far beyond what could happen in reality, by bringing about events which never or very rarely happen in fact. He takes advantage, as it were, of our supposedly surmounted superstitiousness; he deceives us into thinking that he is giving us the sober truth, and then after all oversteps the bounds of possibility. We react to his inventions as we should have reacted to real experiences; by the time we have seen

through his trick it is already too late and the author has
achieved his object; but it must be added that his success
is not unalloyed. We retain a feeling of dissatisfaction, a
kind of grudge against the attempted deceit; I have noticed
this particularly after reading Schnitzler's *Die Weissagung*
and similar stories which flirt with the supernatural. The
writer has then one more means he can use to escape our
rising vexation and at the same time to improve his chances
of success. It is this, that he should keep us in the dark for
a long time about the precise nature of the conditions he
has selected for the world he writes about, or that he
should cunningly and ingeniously avoid any definite information on the point at all throughout the book. Speaking
generally, however, we find a confirmation of the second
part of our proposition—that fiction presents more opportunities for creating uncanny sensations than are possible
in real life.

Strictly speaking, all these complications relate only to
that class of the uncanny which proceeds from forms of
thought that have been surmounted. The class which proceeds from repressed complexes is more irrefragable and
remains as powerful in fiction as in real experience, except
in one point. The uncanny belonging to the first class—
that proceeding from forms of thought that have been surmounted—retains this quality in fiction as in experience
so long as the setting is one of physical reality; but as soon
as it is given an arbitrary and unrealistic setting in fiction,
it is apt to lose its quality of the uncanny.

It is clear that we have not exhausted the possibilities
of poetic licence and the privileges enjoyed by story-
writers in evoking or in excluding an uncanny feeling. In
the main we adopt an unvarying passive attitude towards
experience and are acted upon by our physical environment. But the story-teller has a peculiarly directive influence over us; by means of the states of mind into which
he can put us and the expectations he can rouse in us,
he is able to guide the current of our emotions, dam it up
in one direction and make it flow in another, and he often

obtains a great variety of effects from the same material. All this is nothing new, and has doubtless long since been fully taken into account by professors of aesthetics. We have drifted into this field of research half involuntarily, through the temptation to explain certain instances which contradicted our theory of the causes of the uncanny. And accordingly we will now return to the examination of a few instances.

We have already asked why it is that the severed hand in the story of the treasure of Rhampsenitus has no uncanny effect in the way that Hauff's story of the severed hand has. The question seems to us to have gained in importance now that we have recognized that class of the uncanny which proceeds from repressed complexes to be the more durable of the two. The answer is easy. In the Herodotus story our thoughts are concentrated much more on the superior cunning of the master-thief than on the feelings of the princess. The princess may well have had an uncanny feeling, indeed she very probably fell into a swoon; but we have no such sensations, for we put ourselves in the thief's place, not in hers. In Nestroy's farce, *Der Zerrissene,* another means is used to avoid any impression of the uncanny in the scene in which the fleeing man, convinced that he is a murderer, lifts up one trapdoor after another and each time sees what he takes to be the ghost of his victim rising up out of it. He calls out in despair, "But I've only killed *one* man. Why this horrid multiplication?" We know the truth and do not share the error of the *Zerrissener,* so what must be uncanny to him has an irresistibly comic effect on us. Even a "real" ghost, as in Oscar Wilde's *Canterville Ghost,* loses all power of arousing at any rate an uncanny horror in us as soon as the author begins to amuse himself at its expense and allows liberties to be taken with it. Thus we see how independent emotional effects can be of the actual subject-matter in the world of fiction. In fairy-stories feelings of fear—including uncanny sensations—are ruled out altogether. We understand this, and that is why we ignore the opportunities we find for any development of a feeling of this kind.

Concerning the factors of silence, solitude and darkness, we can only say that they are actually elements in the production of that infantile morbid anxiety from which the majority of human beings have never become quite free. This problem has been discussed from a psycho-analytical point of view in another place.

Dreams and Telepathy (1922)

II

Dreams and Telepathy[1] (1922)

AT THE PRESENT time, when such great interest is felt in what are called "occult" phenomena, very definite anticipations will doubtless be aroused by the announcement of a paper with this title. I will therefore hasten to explain that there is no ground for any such anticipations. You will learn nothing from this paper of mine about the enigma of telepathy; indeed, you will not even gather whether I believe in the existence of "telepathy" or not. On this occasion I have set myself the very modest task of examining the relation of telepathic occurrences, whatever their origin may be, to dreams, more exactly, to our theory of dreams. You will know that the connection between dreams and telepathy is commonly held to be a very intimate one; I shall propound the view that the two have little to do with each other, and that if the existence of telepathic dreams were established there would be no need to alter our conception of dreams in any way.

The material on which the present communication is based is very slight. In the first place, I must express my regret that I could make no use of my own dreams, as I did when I wrote the *Traumdeutung* (1900). But I have never had a "telepathic" dream. Not that I have been without dreams that conveyed an impression of a certain definite occurrence taking place at some distant place, leaving it to the dreamer to decide whether the occurrence is taking place at that moment or will do so at some later time. In waking life, too, I have often become aware of presentiments of distant events. But these hints, foretellings and

[1] Paper read before the Vienna Psychoanalytical Society; published in *Imago*, Bd. viii., 1922. [Translated by C. J. M. Hubback.]

forebodings have none of them "come true," as we say; there proved to be no external reality corresponding to them, and they had therefore to be regarded as purely subjective anticipations.

For example, I once dreamt during the war that one of my sons then serving at the front had fallen. This was not directly stated in the dream, but was expressed in an unmistakable manner, by means of the well-known death-symbolism of which an account was first given by W. Stekel. (Let us not omit here to fulfil the duty, often felt to be inconvenient, of making literary acknowledgements!) I saw the young soldier standing on a landing-stage, between land and water, as it were; he looked to me very pale; I spoke to him but he did not answer. There were other unmistakable indications. He was not wearing military uniform, but a ski-ing costume that he had worn when a serious ski-ing accident had happened to him several years before the war. He stood on something like a footstool with a chest in front of him; a situation always closely associated in my mind with the idea of "falling," through a memory of my own childhood. As a child of little more than two years old I had myself climbed on such a footstool to get something off the top of a chest— probably something good to eat—whereupon I fell and gave myself an injury, of which I can even now show the scar. My son, however, whom the dream pronounced to be dead, came home from the war unscathed.

Only a short time ago, I had another dream announcing misfortune; it was, I think, just before I decided to put together these few remarks. This time there was not much attempt at disguise: I saw my two nieces who live in England; they were dressed in black and said to me "We buried her on Thursday." I knew the reference was to the death of their mother, now eighty-seven years of age, the widow of my eldest brother.

A time of disagreeable anticipation followed; there would of course be nothing surprising in so aged a woman suddenly passing away, yet it would be very unpleasant for the dream to coincide exactly with the occurrence. The next letter from England, however, dissipated this fear. For the benefit of those who are concerned for the wish-fulfilment theory of dreams I may interpolate a reassurance by saying that there was no difficulty in detecting by analysis the unconscious motives that might be presumed to exist in these death-dreams just as in others.

Do not now urge the objection that what I have just related is valueless because negative experiences prove as little here as they do in less occult matters. I am well aware of that and have not adduced these instances with any intention whatever of proving anything or of surreptitiously influencing you in any particular way. My sole purpose was to explain the paucity of my material.

Another fact certainly seems to me of more significance, namely, that during my twenty-seven years of work as an analyst I have never been in a position to observe a truly telepathic dream in any of my patients. The people among whom my practice lay certainly formed a good collection of very neurotic and "highly sensitive" temperaments; many of them have related to me most remarkable incidents in their previous life on which they based a belief in mysterious occult influences. Events such as accidents or illnesses of near relatives, in particular the death of one of the parents, have often enough happened during the treatment and interrupted it; but not on one single occasion did these occurrences, eminently suitable as they were, afford me the opportunity of registering a single telepathic dream, although treatment extended over several months or even years. Anyone may explain this fact as he likes; in any event it again limits the material at my disposal. You will see that any such explanation would not affect the subject of this paper.

Nor does it embarrass me to be asked why I have made no use of the abundant supply of telepathic dreams that have been published. I should not have had far to seek, since the publications of the English as well as of the American Society of Psychical Research are accessible to me as a member of both societies. In all these communications no attempt is ever made to subject such dreams to analytic investigation, which would be our first interest in such cases.[2] Moreover, you will soon perceive that for the purposes of this paper one single dream will serve well enough.

My material thus consists simply and solely of two communications which have reached me from correspondents in Germany. They are not personally known to me, but they give their names and addresses: I have not the least ground for presuming any intention to mislead on the part of the writers.

1

With the first I had already been in correspondence; he had been good enough to send me, as many of my readers do, observations of everyday occurrences and the like. He is obviously an educated and highly intelligent man; this time he expressly places his material at my disposal if I care to turn it "to literary account."

His letter runs as follows:

"I consider the following dream of sufficient interest to give you some material for your researches.

"I must first state the following facts. My daughter, who is married and lives in Berlin, was expecting her first confinement in the middle of December of this year. I intended to go to Berlin about that time with my (second) wife, my daughter's stepmother. During the night of November 16-17 I dreamt, with a vividness and clearness I have never before experienced, that my wife had given birth to twins. I saw quite plainly the two healthy infants with their chubby faces lying in their cot side by side; I was not sure of their sex: one with fair hair had distinctly my features and something of my wife's, the other with chestnut-brown hair clearly resembled her with a look of me. I said to my

[2] In two publications by W. Stekel (mentioned above) (*Der telepathische Traum*, no date, and *Die Sprache des Traumes*, Zweite Auflage, 1922) there are at least attempts to apply the analytic technique to alleged telepathic dreams. The author expresses his belief in the reality of telepathy.

wife, who has red-gold hair, 'Probably "your" child's chestnut hair will also go red later on.' My wife gave them the breast. In the dream she had also made some jam in a washbasin and the two children crept about on all fours in the basin and licked up the contents.

"So much for the dream. Four or five times I had half awaked from it, asked myself if it were true that we had twins, but did not come to the conclusion with any certainty that it was only a dream. The dream lasted till I woke, and after that it was some little time before I felt quite clear about the true state of affairs. At breakfast I told my wife the dream which much amused her. She said, 'Surely Ilse (my daughter) won't have twins?' I answered, 'I should hardly think so, as there have never been twins either in my family or in G.'s' (her husband). On November 18, at ten o'clock in the morning, I received a telegram from my son-in-law handed in the afternoon before, telling me of the birth of twins, boy and girl. The birth thus took place at the time when I was dreaming that my wife had twins. The confinement occurred four weeks earlier than had been expected by my daughter and her husband.

"But there is a further circumstance: the next night I dreamt that my dead wife, my daughter's own mother, had undertaken the care of forty-eight newborn infants. When the first dozen were being brought in, I protested. At that point the dream ended.

"My dead wife was very fond of children. She often talked about it, saying she would like a whole troop round her, the more the better, and that she would do very well if she had charge of a Kindergarten and would be quite happy so. The noise children make was music to her. On one occasion she invited in a whole troop of children from the streets and regaled them with chocolates and cakes in the courtyard of our villa. My daughter must have thought at once of her mother after her confinement, especially because of the surprise of its coming on prematurely, the arrival of twins, and their difference in sex. She knew her mother would have greeted the event with the liveliest joy and sympathy. 'Only think what mother would say, if she were by me now!' This thought must undoubtedly have gone through her mind. And then I dream of my dead wife, of whom I very seldom dream, and had neither spoken of nor thought of since the first dream.

"Do you think the coincidence between dream and event in both cases accidental? My daughter is much attached to me and was most certainly thinking of me during the labour, particularly because we had often exchanged letters during the pregnancy and I had constantly given her advice."

It is easy to guess what my answer to this letter was. I was sorry to find that my correspondent's interest in analysis had been so completely killed by that in telepathy; I therefore avoided his direct question, and, remarking that the dream contained a good deal besides its connection with the birth of the twins, I asked him to let me know what information or incidents could give me a clue to the meaning of the dream.

Thereupon I received the following second letter which certainly did not give me what I wanted:

"I have not been able to answer your kind letter of the 24th until to-day. I shall be only too pleased to tell you 'without omission or reserve' all the associations that occur to me. Unfortunately there is not much, more would come out in talking.

"Well then—my wife and I do not wish for any more children. We very rarely have sexual intercourse; at any rate at the time of the dream there was certainly no 'danger.' My daughter's confinement, which was expected about the middle of December, was naturally a frequent subject of conversation between us. My daughter had been examined and skiagraphed in the summer, and the doctor making the examination had made sure that the child would be a boy. My wife said at the time, 'I should laugh if after all it were a girl.' At the time she also thought to herself it would be better if it were an H. rather than a G. (my son-in-law's family name); my daughter is handsomer and has a better figure than my son-in-law, although he has been a naval officer. I have made some study of the question of heredity and am in the habit of looking at small children to see whom they resemble. One more thing! We have a small dog which sits with us at table in the evening to have his food and licks the plates and dishes. All this material appears in the dream.

"I am fond of small children and have often said that I should like to have the bringing up of a child once more, now that I should have so much more understanding, interest and time to devote to it, but with my wife I should not wish it, as she does not possess the necessary qualities for rearing a child judiciously. The dream makes me a present of two children—I am not sure of the sex. I see them even at this moment lying in the bed and I recognize the features, the one more like myself, the other like my wife, but each with minor traits from the other side. My wife has auburn hair, one of the children chestnut (red) brown. I say, 'Yes, it will later on be red too.' Both the children crawl round a large wash-basin in which my wife has been stirring jam and lick it all over (dream). The origin of this detail is easily explicable, just as is the dream as a whole; it would not be difficult to understand or interpret it, if it had not coincided with the unexpectedly early arrival of my grandchildren (three weeks too soon), a coincidence of time almost to the hour (I cannot exactly say when the dream began; my grandchildren were born at nine P.M. and a quarter past; I went to bed at about eleven and dreamed during the night). Our knowledge too that the child would be a boy adds to the difficulty, though possibly the doubt whether this had been fully established might account for the appearance of twins in the dream. Still, all the same, there is the coincidence of the dream with the unexpected and premature appearance of my daughter's twins.

"It is not the first time that distant events have become known to me before I received the actual news. To give one instance among many. In October I had a visit from my three brothers. We had not all seen one another together for thirty years (naturally one had seen another oftener), once only at my father's funeral and once at my mother's. Both deaths were expected, and I had had no 'presentiments' in either case. But, when about twenty-five years ago my youngest brother died quite suddenly and unexpectedly at the age of nine, as the postman handed me the postcard with the news of his death, before I even glanced at it, the thought came to me at once, 'That is to say that your brother is dead.' He was the only one left at home, a strong healthy lad, while we four elder brothers were already fully fledged and had left the parents' house. At the time of their visit to me the talk by chance came round to this experience of mine, and, as if on the word of command, all three brothers came out with the declaration that exactly the same thing had happened to them. Whether exactly in the same way I cannot say; at all events each one said that he had felt perfectly certain of the death in advance before the quite unexpected news had been communicated, following closely as it did on the presentiment. We are all from the mother's side of a sensitive disposition, though tall, strong men, but not one of us is in the least inclined towards spiritism or occultism; on the contrary, we disclaim adherence to either. My brothers are all three University men, two are schoolmasters, one a surveyor, all rather pedants than visionaries. That is all I can tell you in regard to the dream. If you can turn it to account in any of your writings, I am delighted to place it at your disposal."

I am afraid that you will behave like the writer of these letters. You, too, will be primarily interested in the question whether this dream can really be regarded as a telepathic notification of the unexpected birth of the twin children, and you will not be disposed to submit this dream like any other to analysis. I foresee that it will always be so when psychoanalysis and occultism encounter each other. The former has, so to speak, all our instinctive prepossessions against it; the latter is met half-way by powerful and mysterious sympathies. I am not, however, going to take up the position that I am nothing but a psychoanalyst, that the problems of occultism do not concern me: you would rightly judge that to be only an evasion of the problem. On the contrary, I maintain that it would be a great satisfaction to me if I could convince myself and others on unimpeachable evidence of the existence of telepathic processes, but I also consider that the data about this dream are altogether inadequate to justify any such pronouncement. You will observe that it does not once occur to this intelligent man, deeply interested as he is in the problem of his dream, to tell us when he had last seen his daughter or what news he had lately had from her; he writes in the first letter that the birth was a month too soon, in the second, however, the month has become three weeks only, and in neither do we gain the information whether the birth was really premature, or whether, as so often happens, those concerned were out in their reckoning. But we should have to consider these and other details of the occurrence if we are to weigh the probability of the dreamer making unconscious estimates and guesses. I felt too that it would be of no use even if I succeeded in getting answers to such questions. In the course of arriving at the information new doubts would constantly arise, which could only be set at rest if one had the man in front of one and could revive all the relevant memories which he had perhaps dismissed as unessential. He is certainly right in what he says at the beginning of his second letter: more would come out if he were able to talk to me.

Consider another and similar case, in which the disturbing interest of occultism has no part. You must often have been in the position to compare the anamnesis and the information about the illness given during the first sitting by any neurotic with what you have gained from him after some months of psychoanalysis. Apart from the inevitable abbreviations of the first communication, how many essentials were left out or suppressed, how many displacements made in the relation the various facts bear to one another—in fact, how much that was incorrect or untrue was related to you that first time! You will not call me hypercritical if I refuse in the circumstances to make any pronouncement whether the dream in question is a telepathic fact or a particularly subtle achievement on the part of the dreamer's unconscious or whether it is simply to be taken as a striking coincidence. Our curiosity must be allayed with the hope of some later opportunity for detailed oral examination of the dreamer. But you cannot say that this outcome of our investigation has disappointed you, for I prepared you for it; I said you would hear nothing which would throw any light on the problem of telepathy.

If we now pass on to the analytic treatment of this dream, we are obliged again to admit that we are not satisfied. The material that the dreamer associates with the manifest content of the dream is insufficient to make any analysis possible. The dream, for example, goes into great detail over the likeness of the children to the parents, discusses the colour of their hair and the probable change of colour at a later age, and as an explanation of this much spun-out detail we only have the dry piece of information from the dreamer that he has always been interested in questions of likeness and heredity; we are certainly accustomed to push the matter rather further! But at *one* point the dream does admit of an analytic interpretation, and just at this point analysis, otherwise having no connection with occultism, comes to the aid of telepathy in a remarkable way. It is only on account of this single point that I am asking for your attention to this dream at all.

Rightly viewed, this dream has no right whatever to be called "telepathic." It does not inform the dreamer of anything that is taking place elsewhere—apart from what is otherwise known to him. What, on the other hand, the dream does relate is something quite different from the event reported in the telegram the second day after the night of the dream. Dream and actual occurrence diverge at a particularly important point, and only agree, apart from the coincidence of time, in another very interesting element. In the dream the dreamer's *wife* has twins. The occurrence, however, is that his *daughter* has given birth to twins in her distant home. The dreamer does not overlook this difference, he does not seem to know any way of

getting over it and, as according to his own account he has
no leaning towards the occult, he only asks quite tentatively
whether the coincidence between dream and occurrence
on the point of the twin-birth can be more than an accident.
The psychoanalytic interpretation of dreams, however,
does away with this difference between the dream and the
event, and gives to both the same content. If we consult
the association-material to this dream, it proves to us, in
spite of its sparseness, that an inner bond of feeling exists
between this father and daughter, a bond of feeling which
is so usual and so natural that we ought to cease to be
ashamed of it, one that in daily life merely finds expression
as a tender interest and only in dreams is pushed to its
logical conclusion. The father knows that his daughter
clings to him, he is convinced that she often thought of
him during the labour, in his heart I think he grudges her
to the son-in-law, about whom in one letter he makes a
few disparaging remarks. On the occasion of her confinement (whether expected or communicated by telepathy)
the unconscious though repressed wish becomes active:
"she ought rather to be my (second) wife"; it is this wish
that has distorted the dream-thoughts and is the cause of
the difference between the manifest dream-content and the
event. We are entitled to replace the second wife in the
dream by the daughter. If we possessed more associations
with the dream, we could undoubtedly verify and deepen
this interpretation.

And now I have reached the point I wish to put before
you. We have endeavoured to maintain the strictest im-
partiality and have allowed two conceptions of the dream
to rank as equally probable and equally unproved. According to the first the dream is a reaction to the telepathic
message: "your daughter has just brought twins into the
world." According to the second an unconscious chain of
thought underlies the dream, which may be reproduced
somewhat as follows: "To-day is undoubtedly the day the
confinement will take place if the young people in Berlin
are out in their reckoning by a month, as I strongly suspect.
And if my (first) wife were still alive, she certainly would

not be content with one grandchild! To please her there would have to be at least twins." If this second view is right, no new problems arise. It is simply a dream like any other. The (preconscious) dream-thoughts as outlined above are reinforced by the (unconscious) wish that no other than the daughter should be the second wife of the dreamer, and thus the manifest dream as described to us arises.

If you prefer to assume that a telepathic message about the daughter's confinement reached the sleeper, further questions arise of the relation of such a message to the dream and of its influence on the formation of the dream. The answer is not far to seek and is not at all ambiguous. The telepathic message has been treated as a portion of the material that goes to the formation of a dream, like any other external or internal stimulus, like a disturbing noise in the street or an insistent organic sensation in the sleeper's own body. In our example it is evident how the message, with the help of a lurking repressed wish, becomes remodelled into a wish-fulfilment; it is unfortunately less easy to show that it blends with other material that becomes active at the same time so as to make a dream. The telepathic message—if we are justified in recognizing its existence—can thus make no alteration in the structure of the dream; telepathy has nothing to do with the essential nature of dreams. And that I may avoid the impression that I am trying to conceal a vague notion behind an abstract and fine-sounding word, I am willing to repeat: the essential nature of dreams consists in the peculiar process of the "dreamwork" whereby the preconscious thoughts (residue from the previous day) are worked over into the manifest dream-content by means of an unconscious wish. The problem of telepathy concerns dreams as little as the problem of anxiety.

I am hoping that you will grant this, but that you will raise the objection that there are, nevertheless, other telepathic dreams in which there is no difference between the event and the dream, and in which there is nothing else to be found but the undisguised reproduction of the event.

I have no knowledge of such dreams from my own experience, but I know they have often been reported. If we now assume that we have such an undisguised and unadulterated telepathic dream to deal with, another question arises. Ought we to call such a telepathic experience a "dream" at all? You will certainly do so as long as you keep to popular usage, in which everything that takes place in mental life during sleep is called a dream. You, too, perhaps say, "I tossed about in my dream," and you are not conscious of anything incorrect when you say, "I shed tears in my dream" or "I felt apprehensive in my dream." But notice that in all these cases you are using "dream" and "sleep" and "state of being asleep" interchangeably, as if there were no distinction between them. I think it would be in the interests of scientific accuracy to keep "dream" and "state of sleep" more distinctly separate. Why should we provide a counterpart to the confusion evoked by Maeder who, by refusing to distinguish between the dream-work and the latent dream-thoughts, has discovered a new function for dreams? Supposing, then, that we are brought face to face with a pure telepathic "dream," let us call it instead a telepathic experience in a state of sleep. A dream without condensation, distortion, dramatization, above all, without wish-fulfilment, surely hardly deserves the name. You will remind me that, if so, there are other mental products in sleep to which the right to be called "dreams" would have to be refused. Actual experiences of the day are known to be simply repeated in sleep; reproductions of traumatic scenes in "dreams" have led us only lately to revise the theory of dreams. There are dreams which by certain special qualities are to be distinguished from the usual type, which are, properly speaking, nothing but night-phantasies, not having undergone additions or alterations of any kind and in all other ways similar to the well-known day-dreams. It would be awkward, certainly, to exclude these imaginings from the realm of "dreams." But still they all come from within, are products of our mental life, whereas the very conception of the purely "telepathic dream" lies in its being a perception of something external, in relation to which the mind remains passive and receptive.

2

The second case I intend to bring before your notice belongs to quite another type. This is not a telepathic dream, but a dream that has recurred from childhood onwards, in a person who has had many telepathic experiences. Her letter, which I reproduce here, contains much that is remarkable about which we cannot form any judgement. Some part of it is of interest in connection with the problem of the relation of telepathy to dreams.

1. ". . . My doctor, Herr Dr. N., advises me to give you an account of a dream that has haunted me for about thirty or thirty-two years. I am following his advice, and perhaps the dream may possess interest for you in some scientific respect. Since, in your opinion, such dreams are to be traced to an experience of a sexual nature in the first years of childhood, I relate some reminiscences of childhood, that is, experiences which even now make an impression on me and were of so marked a character as to have determined my religion for me.

"May I beg of you to send me word in what way you explain this dream and whether it is not possible to banish it from my life, for it haunts me like a ghost, and the circumstances that always accompany it—I always fall out of bed, and have inflicted on myself not inconsiderable injuries—make it particularly disagreeable and distressing.

2. "I am thirty-seven years old, very strong and in good physical health, but in childhood I had, besides measles and scarlet fever, an attack of inflammation of the kidneys. In my fifth year I had a very severe inflammation of the eyes, which left double vision. One image slants towards the other and the edges of the image are blurred, as the scars from the ulcers affect the clearness. In the specialist's opinion there is nothing more to be done to the eyes and no chance of improvement. The left side of my face was somewhat awry, from having screwed up my left eye to see better. By dint of practice and determination I can do the

finest needlework, and similarly, when a six-year-old child, I broke myself of squinting sideways by practising in front of a looking-glass, so that now there is no external sign of the defect in vision.

"In my earliest years I was always lonely, kept apart from other children, and had visions (clairvoyance and clairaudience); I was not able to distinguish these from reality, and was often in consequence in embarrassing positions, with the result that I am a very reserved and shy person. Since as a quite small child I already knew far more than I could have learnt, I simply did not understand children of my own age. I am myself the eldest of a family of twelve.

"From six to ten years old I attended the parish school and up to sixteen the high-school of the Ursuline Nuns in B. At ten years old I had taken in as much French in four weeks, in eight lessons, as other children learn in two years. I had only to repeat it and it was just as if I had already learnt it and only forgotten it. I have never had any need to learn French, in contradistinction to English, which certainly gave me no trouble but was not known to me before hand. The same thing happened to me with Latin as with French and I have never properly learnt it, only knowing it from ecclesiastical Latin, which is, however, quite familiar to me. If I read a French book to-day, then I immediately begin thinking in French, whereas this never happens to me with English, although I have more command of English.——My parents are peasant people who for generations have never spoken any languages except German and Polish.

"*Visions:* Sometimes reality vanishes for some moments and I see something quite different. In my house, for example, I often see an old couple and a child; and the house is then differently furnished. In a sanatorium a friend once came into my room at about four in the morning; I was awake, had the lamp burning, and was sitting at my table reading, as I suffer much from sleeplessness. This apparition of her always means a trying time for me—as also on this occasion.

"In 1914 my brother was on active service; I was not with my parents in B., but in C. It was ten in the morning on August 22, when I heard my brother's voice calling, "Mother! mother!" It came again ten minutes later, but I saw nothing. On August 24 I came home, found my mother greatly depressed, and in answer to my questions she said that the boy had appeared on August 22. She had been in the garden in the morning, when she had heard him call, "Mother! mother!" I tried to comfort her and said nothing about myself. Three weeks after there came a card from my brother, written on August 22 between nine and ten in the morning; shortly after that he died.

"On September 27, 1921, while in the sanatorium, I received a message of some kind. There were violent knockings two or three times repeated on the bed of the patient who shared my room. We were both awake; I asked if she had knocked; she had not heard anything at all. Eight weeks later I heard that one of my friends had died in the night of September 26-27.

"Now something which is regarded as an hallucination, a matter of opinion! I have a friend who married a widower with five children; I got to know the husband only through my friend. Nearly every time that I have been to see her, I have seen a lady going in and out of the house. It was natural to suppose that this was the husband's first wife. I asked at some convenient opportunity for a portrait of her, but could not identify the apparition with the photograph. Seven years later I saw a picture with the features of the lady, belonging to one of the children. It was after all the first wife. In the first picture she looked in much better health: she had just been through a feeding-up treatment and that alters the appearance of a consumptive patient.—These are only a few examples out of many.

"*The dream:* I see a tongue of land surrounded by water. The waves are driven to and fro by the surf. On this piece of land stands a palm-tree, bent somewhat towards the water. A woman has her arm wound round the stem of the palm and is bending low towards the water, where a man is trying to reach the shore. At last she lies down on the ground, holds tightly to the palm-tree with her left hand and stretches out her right hand as far as she can towards the man in the water, but without reaching him. At that point I fall out of bed and wake. I was about fifteen or sixteen years old when I realized that this woman was myself, and from that time I not only went through all the woman's apprehensions for the man but I stood there many a time as a third who was not taking part and only looked on. I dreamed this dream too in separate scenes. As the interest in men awoke in me (eighteen to twenty years old), I tried to see the man's face; it was never possible. The foam hid everything but the neck and the back of the head. I have twice been engaged to be married, but the head and build were not those of either of the two men.— Once, when I was living in the sanatorium under the influence of paraldehyde, I saw the man's face, which I now always see in this dream. It was that of the doctor under whose care I was. I liked him as a doctor, but there was nothing more between us.

"*Memories:* Six to nine months old. I was in a perambulator. Quite close to me were two horses; one, a chestnut, is looking at me very hard and in a way full of meaning. This is the most vivid experience; I had the feeling that it was a human being.

"*One year old.* Father and I in the town-park, where a park-keeper is putting a little bird into my hand. Its eyes look into mine. I feel 'That is a live creature like yourself.'

"*Animals being slaughtered.* When I heard the pigs screaming I always called for help and cried out, 'You are killing a person' (four years old). I have always avoided eating meat. Pork always makes me sick. I came to eat meat during the war, but only against my will; now I have given it up again.

"*Five years old.* My mother was confined and I heard her cry out. I had the feeling, 'There is a human being or an animal in the greatest distress,' just as I had over the pig-killing.

"I was quite indifferent as a child to sexual matters; at ten years old I had as yet no conception of offences against chastity. Menstruation came on at the age of twelve. The woman first awakened in me at six-and-twenty, after I had given birth to a child; up to that time (six months) I constantly had violent vomiting after intercourse. This also came on whenever I was at all oppressed in mood.

"I have extraordinarily keen powers of observation, and quite exceptionally sharp hearing, also a very keen sense of smell. I can pick out by smell people I know from among a crowd with my eyes bandaged.

"I do not regard my abnormal powers of sight and hearing as pathological, but ascribe them to finer perceptions and greater quickness of thought; but I have only spoken of it to my pastor and doctor—very unwillingly to the latter, as I was afraid he would tell me that what I regarded as *plus*-qualities were *minus*-qualities, and also because from being misunderstood in childhood I am very reserved and shy."

The dream which the writer of the letter asks us to interpret is not hard to understand. It is a dream of saving from water, a typical birth-dream. The language of symbolism, as you are aware, knows no grammar; it is an extreme case of a language of infinitives, and even the active and passive are represented by one and the same image. If in a dream a woman pulls (or wishes to pull) a man out of the water that may mean she wishes to be his mother (takes him for her son as Pharaoh's daughter did with Moses), or equally she wishes him to make her into a mother, to have a son by him, a son who shall be as like him as a copy. The tree-trunk to which the woman clings is easily recognized as a phallic symbol, even though it is not standing straight up, but inclined towards the surface of the water—in the dream the word is "bent." The onrush and recoil of the surf brought to the mind of another dreamer who was relating a similar dream the comparison with the intermittent pains of labour, and when, knowing that she had not yet borne a child, I asked her how she knew of this characteristic of labour, she said that one imagined labour as a kind of colic, a quite unimpeachable description physiologically. She gave the association "Waves of the

Sea and Waves of Passion."[3] How our dreamer at so early an age can have arrived at the finer details of symbolism: tongue of land, palm-tree, I am naturally unable to say. We must not, however, overlook the fact that, when people maintain that they have for years been haunted by the same dream, it often turns out that the manifest content is not throughout quite the same. Only the kernel of the dream has recurred each time; the details of the content are changed or additions are made to them.

At the end of this dream, which is evidently charged with anxiety, the dreamer falls out of bed. This is a fresh representation of child-birth; analytic investigation of the fear of heights, of the dread of an impulse to throw oneself out of the window, has doubtless led you all to the same conclusion.

Who then is the man, by whom the dreamer wishes to have a child, or of whose very image she would like to be the mother? She has often tried to see his face, but the dream never allows of it; the man has to remain a mystery. We know from countless analyses what this veiling means, and the conclusion we should base on analogy is verified by another statement of the dreamer's. Under the influence of paraldehyde she once recognized the face of the man in the dream as that of the hospital physician who was treating her, and who meant nothing more to her conscious emotional life. The original thus never divulged its identity, but this impression of it in "transference" establishes the conclusion that earlier it must have always been the father. Ferenczi is undoubtedly perfectly right in pointing out that these "dreams of the unsuspecting" are valuable sources of information confirming the conjectures of analysis. Our dreamer was the eldest of twelve children; how often must she have gone through the pangs of jealousy and disappointment when not she, but her mother, obtained from her father the longed-for child!

Our dreamer has quite correctly supposed that her first

[3] [*Des Meeres und der Liebe Wellen*, the title of a play by Grillparzer.]

memories of childhood would be of value in the interpretation of her early and recurrent dream. In the first scene, in
the first year of her life, as she sits in her perambulator she
sees two horses close to her, one looking hard at her in a
significant way. This she describes as her most vivid experience; she had the feeling that it was a human being. This
is a feeling which we can understand only if we assume that
the two horses represent, in this case as so often, man and
wife, father and mother. It is, as it were, a flash of infantile
totemism. If we could, we should ask the writer whether
the *brown* horse who looks at her in so human a way could
not be recognized by its colouring as her father. The second
recollection is associatively connected with the first through
the same "understanding" gaze. "Taking the little bird in
her hand" reminds the analyst, who, by the way, has
prejudices of his own at times, of a feature in the dream
in which the woman's hand is again in contact with another
phallic symbol.

The next two memories belong together; they make still
slighter demands on the interpreter. The mother crying out
during her confinement reminded the daughter directly of
the pigs screaming when they were killed and put her into
the same frenzy of pity. We may also conjecture, however,
that this is a violent reaction against a death-wish directed
at the mother.

With these indications of tenderness for the father, of
contact with his genitals, and of the death-wish against the
mother, the outline of the female Oedipus-complex is
sketched. The ignorance of sexual matters retained so long
and the frigidity at a later period bear out these supposi-
tions. The writer of the letter has been virtually—and for a
time no doubt actually—an hysterical neurotic. The life-
force has, for her own happiness, carried her along with it,
has awakened in her the sexual feelings of a woman and
brought her the joys of motherhood, and the capacity to
work, but a portion of her libido still clings to its point of
fixation in childhood; she still dreams that dream that flings
her out of bed and punishes her for her incestuous object-
choice by "not inconsiderable injuries."

And now a strange doctor's explanation, given in a letter, is to effect something that all the most important experiences of later life have failed to do. Probably a regular analysis continued for a considerable time might have some success. As things were, I was obliged to content myself with writing to her that I was convinced she was suffering from the after-effects of a strong emotional tie binding her to her father and from a corresponding identification with her mother, but that I did not myself expect that this explanation would help her at all. Spontaneous cures of neurosis usually leave scars behind, and these smart from time to time. We are very proud of our art if we achieve a cure through psychoanalysis, yet even so we cannot always prevent the formation of a painful scar in the process.

The little series of reminiscences must engage our attention for a while longer. I have on one occasion stated that such scenes of childhood are "screen-memories" selected at a later period, put together, and thereby not infrequently falsified. This subsequent elaboration serves a purpose that is sometimes easy to guess. In our case one can practically hear the ego of the writer glorifying or soothing itself throughout the whole series of recollections. "I was from a tiny thing a particularly large-hearted and compassionate child. I learnt quite early that the animals have souls as we have, and could not endure cruelty to animals. The sins of the flesh were far from me and I preserved my chastity till late." With declarations such as these she loudly contradicts the inferences that we have to make about her early childhood on the basis of our analytical experience, namely, that she had an abundance of premature sexual emotions and violent feelings of hatred for her mother and her younger brothers and sisters. (Beside the genital significance assigned to it, the little bird may also have that of a child-symbol, like all small animals; her memory also accentuates in a very insistent way that this tiny creature had the same right to exist as she herself.) The short series of recollections in fact furnishes a very nice example of a mental structure with a twofold aspect. Viewed superficially, we may find in it the expression of an abstract idea, here, as usually, with an ethical reference. In H. Silberer's nomenclature the structure has an *anagogic* content; on deeper investigation it reveals itself as a chain of phenomena belonging to the region of the repressed life of the instincts—it displays its *psychoanalytic* content. As you know, Silberer, who was among the first to issue a warning to us on no account to lose sight of the nobler side of the human soul, has put forward the view that all or nearly all dreams permit such a twofold interpretation, a purer, anagogic one beside the ordinary, psychoanalytic one. This is, however, unfortunately not so; on the contrary, a further interpretation of this kind is rarely possible; there has been no valuable example of such a dream-analysis with a double meaning published up to the present time within my knowledge. But something of the kind can often be observed within the series of associations that our patients produce during analytic treatment. The successive ideas are linked on the one hand by an obvious and coherent association, while on the other hand you become aware of an underlying theme which is kept secret and at the same time plays a part in all these ideas. The contrast between the two themes that dominate the same series of ideas is not always one between the lofty anagogic and the common psychoanalytic, but is rather that between shocking and decent or neutral ideas—a fact that easily explains how such a chain of associations with a twofold determination arises. In our present example it is of course not accidental that the anagogic and the psychoanalytic interpretations stand in such a sharp contrast to each other; both relate to the same material, and the later tendency is the same as that seen in the reaction-formations erected against the disowned instinctual forces.

Now why did we make such a special search for the psychoanalytic interpretation instead of contenting ourselves with the more accessible anagogic one? The answer to this is linked up with many other problems—with the existence of neurosis itself and the explanations it inevitably demands—with the fact that virtue does not reward a man with the joy and strength in life that is expected from it, as though it brought with it too much from its original source (this dreamer, too, had not been well rewarded for her virtue), and with many other things which I need not discuss before this audience.

So far, however, in this case we have completely neglected the question of telepathy, the other point of interest in it for us; it is time to return to it. In a sense we have here an easier task than in the case of Herr G. With a person who so easily and so early in life succumbed before reality and replaced it by the world of phantasy, the temptation is irresistible to connect her telepathic experiences and "visions" with her neurosis and to derive them from it, although here too we should not allow ourselves to be deceived as to the cogency of our own arguments. We shall merely replace what is unknown and unintelligible by possibilities that are at least comprehensible.

On August 22, 1914, at ten o'clock in the morning, our correspondent experienced a telepathic impression that her brother, who was at the time on active service, was calling, "Mother! mother!"; the phenomenon was purely acoustic, it was repeated shortly after, but nothing was seen. Two days later she sees her mother and finds her much depressed because the boy had announced himself to her by repeatedly calling, "Mother! mother!" She immediately recalls the same telepathic message, which she had experienced at the same time, and as a matter of fact some weeks later it was established that the young soldier had died on that day at the hour stated.

It cannot be proved, but also cannot be disproved, that instead of this what happened was the following: the mother told her one day that the son had sent this telepathic message; whereupon the conviction at once arose in her mind that she had had the same experience at the same time. Such delusory memories arise in the mind with the force of an obsession, a force derived from real sources— they have, however, substituted material for psychical reality. The strength of the delusory memory lies in its being an excellent way of expressing the sister's tendency to identify herself with the mother. "You are anxious about the boy, but I am really his mother, and his cry was meant for me; I had this telepathic message." The sister would naturally firmly decline to consider our attempt at explanation and would hold to her belief in the authenticity of the experience. She simply cannot do otherwise; as long as the reality of the unconscious basis of it in her own mind is concealed from her she is obliged to believe in the reality of her pathological logic. Every such delusion derives its strength and its unassailable character from its source in unconscious psychical reality. I note in passing that it is not incumbent on us here to explain the mother's experience or to investigate its authenticity.

The dead brother is, however, not only the imaginary child of our correspondent; he represents also a rival regarded with hatred even at the time of his birth. By far the greater number of all telepathic presentiments relate to death or the possibility of death: when patients under analysis keep telling us of the frequency and infallibility of their gloomy forebodings, we can with equal regularity show them that they are fostering particularly strong death-wishes in their unconscious against their nearest relations and have therefore long suppressed them. The patient whose history I related in 1909[4] was an example to the point; he was even called a "bird of ill omen" by his relations. But when the kindly and highly intelligent man—who has since himself perished in the war—began to make progress towards recovery, he himself gave me considerable assistance in clearing up his own psychological conjuring tricks. In the same way, the account given in our first correspondent's letter, of how he and his three brothers had received the news of their youngest brother's death as a thing they had long been inwardly aware of, appears to need no other explanation. The elder brothers would all have been equally convinced of the superfluousness of the youngest arrival.

Another of our dreamer's "visions" will probably be-

[4] "Notes upon a Case of Obsessional Neurosis," *Three Case Histories*, Collier Books edition BS 191V.

come more intelligible in the light of analytical knowledge! Women friends have obviously a considerable significance in her emotional life. News of the death of one of them is conveyed to her shortly after the event by knocking at night on the bed of a room-mate in the sanatorium. Another friend had many years before married a widower with several (five) children. On the occasion of her visits to their house she regularly saw the apparition of a lady, whom she felt constrained to suppose to be the dead first wife; this did not at first permit of confirmation, and only became a matter of certainty with her seven years later, on the discovery of a fresh photograph of the dead woman. This achievement in the way of a vision has the same inner dependence on the family-complex already recognized in our correspondent as her presentiment of the brother's death. By identifying herself with her friend she could in her person achieve her own wish-fulfilment; for all eldest daughters of a numerous family build up in their unconscious the phantasy of becoming the father's second wife by the death of the mother. If the mother is ill or dies, the eldest daughter takes her place as a matter of course in relation to the younger brothers and sisters, and may even in respect to the father take over some part of the functions of the wife. The unconscious wish fills in the other part.

I am now almost at the end of what I wish to say. I might, however, add the observation that the cases of telepathic messages or occurrences which have been discussed here are clearly connected with emotions belonging to the sphere of the Oedipus-complex. This may sound startling; I do not intend to give it out as a great discovery, however. I would rather revert to the result we arrived at through investigating the dream I considered first. Telepathy has no relation to the essential nature of dreams; it cannot deepen in any way what we already understand of them by analysis. On the other hand, psychoanalysis may do something to advance the study of telepathy, in so far as, by the help of its interpretations, many of the puzzling characteristics of telepathic phenomena may be rendered more intelligible to us; or other, still doubtful phenomena be for the first time definitely ascertained to be of a telepathic nature.

There remains one element of the apparently intimate connection between telepathy and dreams which is not affected by any of these considerations: namely, the incontestable fact that sleep creates favourable conditions for telepathy. Sleep is not, it is true, indispensable to the accomplishment of the process—whether it originates in messages or in an unconscious activity of some kind. If you are not already aware of this, you will learn it from the instance given by our second correspondent, of the message coming from the boy between nine and ten in the morning. We must add, however, that no one has a right to take exception to telepathic occurrences on the ground that the event and the presentiment (or message) do not exactly coincide in astronomical time. It is perfectly conceivable that a telepathic message might arrive contemporaneously with the event and yet only penetrate to consciousness the following night during sleep (or even in waking life only after a while, during some pause in the activity of the mind). We are, as you know, of opinion that dream-formation itself does not necessarily wait for the onset of sleep to begin. Often the latent dream-thoughts may have been lying ready during the whole day, till at night they find the contact with the unconscious wish that shapes them into a dream. But if the phenomenon of telepathy is only an activity of the unconscious mind, then no fresh problem lies before us. The laws of unconscious mental life may then be taken for granted as applying to telepathy.

Have I given you the impression that I am secretly inclined to support the reality of telepathy in the occult sense? If so, I should very much regret that it is so difficult to avoid giving such an impression. In reality, however, I was anxious to be strictly impartial. I have every reason to be so, for I have no opinion; I know nothing about it.

A Neurosis of Demonical Possession in the Seventeenth Century (1923)

III

A Neurosis of Demonical Possession in the Seventeenth Century[1] (1923)

EXPERIENCE OF NEUROSES amongst children goes to show that in them much is clearly visible to the naked eye which at a later age can only be discovered after painstaking research. We may anticipate that the same holds true for the neurotic manifestations characteristic of earlier centuries, provided, of course, that we are prepared to recognize them as such under other names than those of our present-day neuroses. When we consider how in our present unpsychological epoch neuroses appear in a hypochondriacal guise, masked as organic diseases, we need not be surprised to find the neuroses of olden times masquerading in a demonological shape. As is known, many authors, foremost amongst them Charcot, have recognized states of demoniacal possession and ecstasy, descriptions of which have been preserved for us in the artistic productions of those periods, to be manifestations of hysteria; had more attention been paid to the history of such cases at the time, it would have been a simple matter to find in them the same content as that of the neuroses to-day.

Despite the somatic ideology of the era of "exact" science, the demonological theory of these dark ages has in the long run justified itself. Cases of demoniacal possession correspond to the neuroses of the present day; in order to understand these latter we have once more had recourse

[1] First published in *Imago*, Bd. ix., 1923. [Translated by Edward Glover.]

The author wishes to add to the English translation two footnotes (which appear within square brackets), and to express his regret that they were omitted from the German version.

to the conception of psychic forces. What in those days were thought to be evil spirits to us are base and evil wishes, the derivatives of impulses which have been rejected and repressed. In one respect only do we not subscribe to the explanation of these phenomena current in mediaeval times; we have abandoned the projection of them into the outer world, attributing their origin instead to the inner life of the patient in whom they manifest themselves.

1. THE STORY OF CHRISTOPH HAITZMANN, THE PAINTER

I am indebted to the friendly interest of Hofrat Dr. R. Payer-Thurn, director of the former Imperial *Fideikommissbibliothek* of Vienna for the opportunity of studying one of these demonological neuroses, which occurred in the seventeenth century. This gentleman discovered in the Imperial Library a manuscript originating from Mariazell, a place of pilgrimage, in which was described in detail how a pact with the Devil had been redeemed in a wonderful manner through the interposition of the Holy Virgin Mary. His interest was aroused by the resemblance of this story to the Faust legend, and led him to undertake a comprehensive presentation of the material. Finding, however, that the person whose redemption was described had been subject to visions and convulsive seizures, Dr. Payer-Thurn turned to me for a medical opinion on the case. In the end we agreed to publish our investigations independently and apart. I wish to take this opportunity of thanking him for his suggestion and for his assistance in various ways in studying the manuscript.

The history of this demonological neurosis leads to a really valuable discovery, which can be brought to light without much interpretative work—much as a vein of pure metal may sometimes be struck when elsewhere the ore can only be extracted after laborious smelting operations.

The manuscript, an exact duplicate of which is in my possession, consists of two parts entirely distinct from each other: one written in Latin by a monastic author or compiler, and the other a fragment from the patient's diary written in German. The former contains a preface and a description of the actual miracle; the latter can scarcely have been of much interest to the clerics but is all the more valuable to us. It serves in large part to confirm our otherwise tentative views on the case, and we have every reason to be grateful to the reverend fathers for having preserved the document although it contributed nothing of value from their point of view; indeed, rather the contrary.

Before summarizing the contents of this little handwritten brochure, which bears the title *Trophaeum Mariano-Cellense*, I must narrate a part of its contents which I take from the Preface.

On September 5, 1677, the painter Christoph Haitzmann, a native of Bavaria, was brought to Mariazell bearing a letter of introduction from the Pastor of Pottenbrunn (in Lower Austria), which lies not far away.[2] For some months he had lived in Pottenbrunn pursuing his occupation of painting; on August 29, whilst in church, he was seized with frightful convulsions and, as these recurred in the days following, he had been interrogated by the Praefectus Dominii Pottenbrunnensis, in order to discover what was oppressing him and whether he had yielded to an impulse to have illicit traffic with the Evil One.[3] Whereupon he confessed that nine years previously, in a state of despondency in regard to his art and of despair about his livelihood, he had succumbed to the nine-times-repeated temptation of the Evil One and had given his bond in writing to belong to the Devil body and soul at the end of nine years. On the twenty-fourth of that month the period would expire.[4] The unfortunate man had rued

[2] No mention is anywhere made of the painter's age. One surmises from the context that he was between thirty and forty, probably nearer thirty. He died, as we shall hear, in 1700.

[3] We can only note here in passing the possibility that this cross-examination of the patient "suggested" to him the phantasy of a pact with the Devil.

[4] *Quorum et finis 24 mensis hujus futurus appropinquat.*

his bargain and was convinced that only the grace of the Mother of God at Mariazell could save him, by compelling the Evil One to disgorge this Bond which was written in blood. On these grounds he (*miserum hunc hominem omni auxilio destitutum*) had been consigned to the benevolence of the fathers of Mariazell.

So far the story of Leopoldus Braun, Pastor of Pottenbrunn, September 1, 1677.

To come now to the analysis of the Manuscript. It consists of three parts:

(1) A coloured title-page representing the scenes of the signing of the Pact and of the redemption in the shrine of Mariazell; on the next page are eight drawings, likewise coloured, representing subsequent appearances of the Devil, with a brief legend in German attached to each. These illustrations are not original; they are copies—exact copies, we are solemnly assured—from original paintings by Christoph Haitzmann.

(2) The actual *Trophaeum Mariano-Cellense* (in Latin), the work of a reverend compiler who signs himself at the foot P. A. E., adding four lines in verse containing his biography. It ends with a deposition by the Abbot Kilian of St. Lambert, dated September 12, 1729, which is in a different handwriting, and testifies to the exact correspondence of manuscript and illustrations with the originals preserved in the archives. The year in which the *Trophaeum* was written is not mentioned. We are at liberty to assume that it was done in the same year as that in which the Abbot Kilian made his deposition, in 1729; or, since 1714 is the last date mentioned in the text, we may put the work of the compiler somewhere between 1714 and 1729. The miracle which has been rescued from oblivion by means of this manuscript happened in the year 1677, that is to say, from thirty-seven to fifty-two years before.

(3) The painter's diary written in German, covering the period from his redemption in the shrine until January 13 in the following year, 1678. It is inserted in the text of the *Trophaeum* almost at the end.

The main part of the actual *Trophaeum* is made up of

two portions, the before-mentioned letter of introduction of the Pastor of Pottenbrunn, Leopold Braun, dated September 1, 1677, and the report of the Abbot Franciscus of Mariazell and St. Lambert describing the miraculous cure, dated September 12, 1677, that is to say, only a few days after it happened. The work of the editor or compiler P. A. E. consists of a preface in which the contents of these two documents are condensed, together with some less important passages introduced to connect the two, and a report at the end on the subsequent history of the painter based on inquiries made in the year 1714.[5]

The painter's previous history is thus related three times over in the *Trophaeum*: (1) in the introductory letter from the Pastor of Pottenbrunn, (2) in the formal deposition of the Abbot Franciscus and (3) in the editorial preface. A comparison of these three sources discloses certain contradictions which it will be important for us to follow up.

I can now continue the story of the painter. After a prolonged period of expiation and prayer at Mariazell, the Devil appeared before him in the Holy Shrine at midnight on September 8, the birthday of the Virgin, in the form of a winged dragon, and gave him back the Pact, which was written in blood. Much to our surprise we learn at a later stage that two Pacts with the Devil are mentioned in the history of Christoph Haitzmann, an earlier one written in black ink and a later one written in blood. The one referred to in the scene of exorcism, which is also that illustrated on the title-page, is the Blood Pact, that is, the later one.

It might occur to us at this point to question the credibility of these ecclesiastical reporters—a misgiving prompting us not to waste our energies on a mere product of monastic superstition. We are told that several clerics, each mentioned by name, assisted at the exorcism and were even present in the chapel during the Devil's appearance. Now had it been stated that they had also witnessed the

---

[5] This would seem to indicate that the *Trophaeum* too was written in the year 1714.

dragon delivering to the painter this document inscribed in red (*schedam sibi porrigentem conspexisset*), we should be confronted by several disturbing possibilities, the least disagreeable of which would be that of a collective hallucination. The testimony of the Abbot Franciscus, however, dispels this misgiving. It is nowhere stated that the clergy present saw the Devil; on the contrary, it is quite frankly and soberly recorded that the painter tore himself from the arms of the fathers who were supporting him, rushed into the corner of the chapel where he saw the apparition and returned with the Bond in his hand.[6]

It was a wonderful miracle; the triumph of the Holy Mother over Satan was beyond all question, but unfortunately the cure was not a permanent one. It is again to the credit of the churchmen that they do not conceal this. After a brief interval the painter left Mariazell in good health and proceeded to Vienna, where he lived with a married sister. On October 11 fresh seizures occurred, some of them very severe, and these are reported in the Diary until January 13. They took the form of visions and of loss of consciousness, during which he saw and experienced all manner of things; also of convulsive seizures accompanied by extremely painful sensations; on one occasion paralysis of the lower limbs occurred; and so on. This time it was not the Devil, however, who persecuted him; on the contrary, these unwelcome attentions came from sacred personages, Christ and the Holy Virgin herself. It is remarkable that he suffered no less from the visitations of these heavenly persons and from the penances they imposed on him than from his former traffic with the Devil. We discover from the Diary that he regarded these fresh manifestations as Satanic apparitions too, and when in May 1678 he went back to Mariazell we find him bewailing these *maligni Spiritus manifestationes.*

[6] . . . *ipsumque Daemonem ad Aram Sac. Cellae per fenestrellam in cornu Epistolae Schedam sibi porrigentem conspexisset eo advolans e Religiosorum manibus, qui eum tenebant, ipsam Schedam ad manum obtinuit.* . . .

He explained to the reverend fathers that he had come back in order to recover from the Devil a still earlier Pact written in ink.[7] Again this time the Holy Virgin and the pious fathers helped him to obtain the answer to his prayer. As to how this came about, however, the report is silent. It says briefly: *qua iuxta votum reddita*. Once again he prayed, and once again the Pact was returned to him. Afterwards he felt quite free and entered the Order of Monks Hospitallers.

We have once more to acknowledge that, despite the quite obvious tendency behind his work, the compiler has not been tempted into departing from that veracity which is a condition of a clinical history. When in 1714 inquiry is made of the Superior of the Cloister of Monks Hospitallers concerning the painter's after-history, the information obtained is not suppressed. Reverendus Pater Provincialis reports that Brother Chrysostomus had again been repeatedly tempted by the Evil One, who wished to strike a fresh Pact with him: and indeed, that this occurred only when "he had taken somewhat more wine than usual,"[8] but by the grace of God it had always been possible for him to repulse these approaches. In the year 1700, in the cloister of the Order at Neustatt on Moldau, Brother Chrysostomus, "meek in spirit and of good comfort," died of a fever.

2. THE MOTIVATION OF THE SATANIC PACT

When we come to consider this Bond with Satan as if it were the case-history of a neurotic, our interest is aroused in the first instance by the problem of its motivation, which is of course closely connected with the question of its exciting cause. Why does one sell oneself to the Devil? To be sure, Dr. Faust puts the contemptuous question: What hast thou to give, thou poor Devil? But he erred; the Devil,

---

[7] This had been drawn up in September 1668, and in May 1678, nine and a half years after, would have been long overdue.

[8] *"Wenn er etwas mehrers von Wein getrunken."*

in return for the immortal soul, has much to offer that is highly treasured of man: wealth, immunity from dangers, power over mankind and over the forces of Nature, but above all these, pleasure, the enjoyment of beautiful women. Moreover, in pacts with the Devil these terms or obligations are usually specifically mentioned.[9] What then was Christoph Haitzmann's reason for entering into his Bond?

Remarkable to relate, it was not for any one of these very natural desires. To put the matter beyond all doubt, one has only to read the brief remarks appended by the artist to his illustrations of the apparitions of the Devil. For example, the legend appended to the Third Vision runs:

Zum driten ist er mir in anderthalb Jahren in disser abscheühlichen Gestalt erschinen, mit einen Buuch in der Handt, darin lauter Zauberey und schwarze Kunst war begrüffen . . .

[For the third time within one yeare and a half he hath appeared vnto me in this loathsome shape bearing in his hand a Booke the which is full of naught but wizardrie and blacke magicke.]

We learn, however, from the legend under a later apparition that the Devil reproaches him furiously for having "burnt his aforetold Booke" and threatens to tear him to pieces if he does not bring it him back.

In the Fourth Vision he shows him a large yellow money-bag and a great ducat, promising to give him as many of these as he cares to have: the painter, however, can boast of his reply, "but I would in no wise accept of such things."

On another occasion the Devil demands that he should turn to pleasure and amusement, concerning which the painter remarks, "*welliches zwar auch auf sein begehren*

[9] Cf. *Faust*, I.   Study.
> I'll pledge myself to be your servant *here*,
> Ne'er at your call to slumber or be still;
> But when together *yonder* we appear,
> You shall submissively obey my will.
>   (Translation by Anna Swanwick.)

geschehen aber ich yber drey Tag nit continuirt, und gleich widerumb aussgelöst worden" [the which on his entreatie did come to pass, yet did I not continue for more than three days and was speedilie redeemed anew].

Now since he refuses magical powers, money and pleasure when the Devil offers them, and still less makes them a condition of the Bond, it becomes really imperative to know what the painter desired of the Devil when he entered into the Pact. Some motive or other he must have had to induce him to have any such dealings at all.

On this point, too, the *Trophaeum* provides us with reliable information. He had become depressed, was unable or unwilling to paint properly and was anxious about his livelihood, that is to say, he suffered from melancholic depression with incapacity for work and (justified) anxiety about his future. It is clear that we are really dealing with a morbid state of health, and further, we are informed of the exciting cause of the disease; the painter himself, in the legends appended to his illustrations, actually describes it as a melancholia ("that I should seeke diversion and banish Melancholy"). The first of our three sources of information, the letter of introduction from the Pastor, to be sure, speaks only of the depression (*"dum artis suae progressum emolumentumque secuturum* PUSILLANIMIS *perpenderet"*); the second source, however, the report of the Abbot Franciscus, indicates the cause of this despondency or depression: it runs thus: *"accepta aliqua pusillanimitate* EX MORTE PARENTIS,*"* and in the compiler's introduction the same reason is advanced, merely the order of the wording being inverted: *ex morte parentis accepta aliqua pusillanimitate*. That is to say, his father had died and he had consequently fallen into a state of melancholia, whereupon the Devil had appeared before him, inquired the cause of his dejection and grief, and had promised "to help him in every way and give him aid."[10]

---

[10] *"Auf alle Weiss zu helfen und an die Handt zu gehen."* The first picture on the title-page, and its legend, shows the Devil in the form of an *"ersamer Bürger"* (honest burgher).

This man sold himself to the Devil, therefore, in order to be freed from a state of depression. Truly an excellent motive, in the judgement of those who can understand the torment of these states and who appreciate, moreover, how little the art of medicine can do to alleviate the malady. Yet I question if a single one of my readers who has followed the tale thus far could guess the wording of the Pact, or rather Pacts (since there are two, one written in ink and a second written about a year later in blood, both presumably still in the archives at Mariazell, and transcribed in the *Trophaeum*).

These agreements hold two great surprises in store for us. First of all there is no mention in either of them that it was for certain obligations to be fulfilled by the Devil that the painter had bartered eternal bliss: there is but one condition, which the Devil makes and the painter must observe. It strikes us as being entirely illogical and absurd that this man should barter his soul, not for something which the Devil shall afford him, but for a service which he shall himself render to the Devil. The actual agreement made by the painter sounds more extraordinary still.

The First "Syngrapha," written in black ink:

Ich Christoph Haitzmann undterschreibe mich diesen Herrn sein leibeigener Sohn auff 9 Jahr

1669 Jahr.

[*I Christoph Haitzmann sign a deede and pledge myselfe to be vnto this lord euen as a sonne of his bodie for 9 yeares.*   *1669 yeare*]

The Second, written in blood:

Anno 1669 Christoph Haizmann Ich verschreibe mich dissen Satan, ich sein leibeigner Sohn zu sein, vnd in 9 Jahr ihm mein Leib und Seel zuzugeheren

[*Anno 1669 Christoph Haizmann I give my bonde and pledge myselfe vnto this Satan for to be vnto him euen as a sonne of his bodie and after 9 yeares to belong vnto him bodie and saule*]

Our astonishment vanishes, however, when we read the text in the sense that what appears to be a service demanded of the painter by Satan is instead an obligation on the part of Satan towards the painter. This incomprehensible Pact would then acquire a straightforward meaning which might be expressed thus: The Devil binds himself for a period of nine years to take the place of his lost father to the painter. At the end of this period the latter, as was customary in such dealings, becomes the property of the Devil body and soul. The train of thought motivating this Pact seems indeed to be as follows: Owing to my father's death I am despondent and can no longer work; if I can but get a father-substitute I shall be able to regain all that I have lost.

A man who has fallen into a melancholia on account of his father's death must have loved that father deeply. The more curious then that he should have come by the idea of taking the Devil as a substitute for the loved parent.

3. THE DEVIL AS A FATHER-SUBSTITUTE

I daresay sober-minded critics will not be prepared to admit that by reversing the sense of this Satanic Pact we have made the matter clear. Two objections to this procedure might be advanced. In the first place, it might be said that it is unnecessary to regard the Pact as a contract in which the obligations of both parties are set forth. It might contain merely the painter's obligations, without any reference in the text to the obligations of the Devil, which would remain "understood." The painter, however, binds himself in two ways, first to be as a son to the Devil for nine years, and secondly, to belong to him entirely after death. In this way one of the premises on which our conclusion is based would be disposed of.

The burden of the second objection would be that there is no justification for laying stress on the expression, "the son of his body." This is merely a phrase current at that time, which could quite well be interpreted in the way the reverend fathers understood it. The latter did not translate into Latin the kinship laid down in the Pact, but merely say that the painter "*mancipavit*" himself to the Evil One, surrendered himself to him, had taken upon himself to lead a life of wickedness and to deny God and the Holy Trinity.

Why should we hold aloof from this obvious and natural explanation?[11] The state of affairs would then simply be that someone in a helpless state, tortured with melancholic depression, sells himself to the Devil, in whose healing powers he reposes the greatest confidence. That the depression was caused by the father's demise would then be quite irrelevant: it could quite conceivably have been due to some other cause. This seems a forceful and reasonable objection. We hear once more the familiar criticism of psychoanalysis that it regards the simplest affairs in an unduly subtle and complicated way, discovers secrets and problems where none exist, and that it achieves this by magnifying the most insignificant trifles to support far-reaching and bizarre conclusions. It would be fruitless to assure our opponents that this rejection on their part involves the neglect of many striking analogies and the breaking of many delicate connecting-threads, such as we can point to in the present instance. Our opponent would merely reply that such analogies and connecting-links were nonexistent, that they were artifacts introduced by ourselves, figments of our overweening sagacity.

Now I shall not preface my reply with the words, "Let us be honest" or "Let us be sincere," since that one must always be able to be, and without making any preliminary flourish about it. Let me say quite simply that I am well aware that any reader who does not already believe in the soundness of the psychoanalytic mode of thought will certainly not acquire this conviction by reading the case of Christoph Haitzmann, painter in the seventeenth century. Nor is it my intention to put forward this case as a proof of the validity of psychoanalytic findings: on the contrary, I presuppose their soundness and I then make use of them to explain this painter's demonological disease.

[11] As a matter of fact, when we come to consider when and for whom these Pacts were drawn up, we shall realize that the text had of necessity to read inoffensively and in comprehensible terms. It suffices for our purposes, however, that some ambiguity should be contained in them, which we can make the starting-point of our investigations.

My justification for so doing lies in the success of our investigations into the nature of the neuroses in general. Speaking in all modesty, we may venture to say that even the more obtuse amongst our colleagues and contemporaries are beginning to realize that no understanding of neurotic states is to be attained without the help of psychoanalysis.

With these shafts alone can Troy be taken.

as Odysseus admits in the *Philoctetes* of Sophocles.

If we are right in regarding as a neurotic phantasy the Satanic Pact made by our painter, there is no further need to apologize for interpreting it psychoanalytically. Even trifling indications have meaning and significance, and especially as regards the causal conditions of a neurosis. To be sure, it is possible to overvalue them, just as it is to underestimate them; it remains a matter of judgement how far one should go in relying on them. But if a person does not believe in psychoanalysis, nor even in the Devil, he must be left to make what he can of the painter's case, whether he fashion an explanation by some means of his own or whether he sees nothing at all in the case deserving of explanation.

We will come back, therefore, to our assumption that the Devil to whom the painter sells himself is a direct father-substitute. In keeping with this is the shape in which he makes his first appearance: an honest old burgher with a flowing brown beard, dressed in a red mantle with a black hat, leaning on a stick in his right hand, and beside him a black hound (Picture 1).[12] The forms he assumes after become ever more terrifying, one might almost say more mythological: he is decked out with horns, eagle's talons, and bat's wings; finally he appears in the shrine as a flying dragon. We shall have occasion to return later to a particular detail of his bodily shape.

[12] In Goethe a black dog like this turns into the Devil himself.

It does indeed sound strange that the Devil should be chosen as a substitute for a loved father, but only when we hear of this for the first time; there are many facts at our disposal which can serve to temper our astonishment. First of all we know that God is a father-substitute, or more correctly, an exalted father, or yet again, a reproduction of the father as seen and met with in childhood— as the individual sees him in his own childhood and as mankind saw him in prehistoric times in the father of the primal horde. Later on in life the individual acquired a different, a less exalted impression of him, but the childish image of him was preserved and it united with the inherited memory-traces of the primal father to form the idea of God. We know, too, from the inner life of individuals as disclosed in analysis, that the relation to this father was in all probability ambivalent from the outset, or at any rate it soon became so; that is to say, it comprised two sets of emotional impulses, quite opposite in nature, not merely one of fondness and submission but another of hostility and defiance. We hold that this ambivalence governs the relations of mankind to its deities. From this unresolved conflict, on the one hand of longing for the father and on the other of dread and defiance, we have explained some of the important characteristics and most epoch-making vicissitudes of religion.[13]

Concerning the Evil Spirit, we know that he is regarded as the antithesis of God, yet as being somewhat akin to him in nature. His history has not been gone into so closely as has that of God: not all religions have adopted the Evil One, the enemy of God; and his prototype in individual life remains as yet obscure. One thing, however, is certain: gods can turn into evil spirits when new gods supplant them. When one people vanquishes another, the overthrown gods of the conquered become not infrequently the evil spirits of the victors. The evil spirit of the Christian faith, the Devil of mediaeval times, was accord-

---

[13] Cf. Freud, *Totem und Tabu,* and, in detail, Theodor Reik, *seiner Beziehung zu gewissen Formen des mittelälterlichen*

ing to Christian mythology, himself a fallen angel of god-like nature. It requires no great analytic insight to divine that God and the Devil were originally one and the same, a single figure which was later split into two bearing opposed characteristics.[14] In the prehistoric age of the religions, all those terrifying features which were afterwards merged in the form of his counterpart were still borne by the god himself.

It is an example of the process, so familiar to us, by which an idea with an opposed—ambivalent—content is split into two opposites contrasting sharply. The antitheses contained in the original idea of the nature of God are but a reflection of the ambivalence governing the relation of an individual to his personal father. If the benevolent and righteous God is a father-substitute, it is not to be wondered at that the hostile attitude, which leads to hate, fear and accusations against him, comes to expression in the figure of Satan. The father is thus the individual prototype of both God and the Devil. The fact that the figure of the primal father was that of a being with unlimited potentialities of evil, bearing much more resemblance to the Devil than to God, must have left an indelible stamp on all religions.

To be sure, it is by no means easy to demonstrate in the mental life of the individual traces of this satanic conception of the father. When a boy takes to drawing caricatures and grotesque figures, it may be possible to prove that he is making a mock of his father; nor is it difficult, when children of both sexes are apprehensive at night about robbers and burglars, to recognize these as derivatives of the father.[15] The animals which play a part in the animal-phobias of children are generally father-substitutes, just as the totem animal was in primitive times. But that the Devil

[14] Cf. Theodor Reik, "Gott und Teufel," *Der eigene und der fremde Gott* [quoting Ernest Jones, *Der Alptraum in seiner Beziehung zu gewissen Formen des mittelälterlichen Aberglaubens*. See footnote p. 91].

[15] In the familiar tale of the Seven Little Goats, Father Wolf appears as a burglar.

is an image of the father and can act as an understudy for him has never been so clearly apparent as in the case of our neurotic seventeenth-century painter. It was this that, at the beginning of this paper, led me to express my belief that a demonological record of this kind would furnish that pure metal which, in the neuroses of a later age—no longer superstitious but rather hypochondriacal—can only be extracted from the raw ore of symptoms and associations by a laborious analytic process.[16]

Closer analysis of this case will in all probability bring deeper conviction. It is no unusual thing for a man to develop melancholic depression and loss of power to work after the death of his father. We conclude that such persons have been attached to the father with bonds of deep affection and are reminded how often a severe melancholia appears as a neurotic form of grief.

So far we are undoubtedly right, but not if we suppose further that the relation has been merely one of love. On the contrary, the more ambivalent the relation had been, the more likely is the grief for the father's loss to turn into a melancholia. When we bring this ambivalence into the foreground, however, we become prepared for the possibility of the father being denigrated in such a way as comes to ex-

---

[16] The fact that we so seldom in analyses find the Devil figuring as a father-substitute probably indicates that, in those we analyse, the rôle of this mediaeval, mythological figure has long since been outplayed. It was just as much the duty of a pious Christian in earlier centuries to believe in the Devil as to believe in God. As a matter of fact, the Devil was necessary in order to make him cling fast to God. For various reasons the increase in scepticism has affected first and foremost the person of the Devil.

Once one brings oneself to regard this idea of the Devil in the part of father-substitute as a phenomenon of cultural development, a fresh light dawns on the witch-trials of the Middle Ages [as has already been shown by Ernest Jones in the chapter on "Die Hexenepidemie" in his *Der Alptraum in seiner Beziehung zu gewissen Formen des mittelälterlichen Aberglaubens*. See footnote p. 91].

pression in the painter's demoniacal neurosis. If only we were in a position to learn as much about Christoph Haitzmann as we do of patients undergoing analysis, it would be a simple matter to develop this ambivalence, to bring into memory when and how he had cause to fear and hate his father, above all, to discover the accidental factors present in addition to the usual motives for father-hate which are inevitable in the natural father-son relation. The inhibition of working capacity, for example, might have had some special explanation. It is possible that the father had opposed his son's wish to become a painter; his incapacity to paint after the father's death would then, on the one hand, be an expression of the familiar "deferred obedience"; and, on the other, by rendering him incapable of making a livelihood it would be bound to increase his longing for the father to stand between him and the cares of life. As deferred obedience it would also constitute an expression of remorse and a successful self-punishment.

Since, however, we cannot set about the personal analysis of Christoph Haitzmann, *obiit* 1700, we must content ourselves with drawing special attention to such features in his clinical history as suggest typical exciting causes for the negative attitude to the father. There are not many such, nor are they particularly obvious, nevertheless such details as do exist are highly interesting.

Consider first of all the part played by the number Nine. The Bond with the Evil One was for nine years. On this point the entirely trustworthy report of the Pastor of Pottenbrunn is quite clear: *pro novem annis Syngraphen scriptam tradidit.* This letter, dated September 1, 1677, also informs us that the appointed term was about to expire in a few days: *quorum et finis 24 mensis hujus futurus appropinquat.* The Pact would therefore have been drawn up on September 24, 1668.[17] In the same report, indeed, yet another use is made of the number nine. *Nonies*—nine times—did the painter withstand the temptations of the

---

[17] The contradiction disclosed by the fact that both the Pacts transcribed bear the date 1669 will be considered later.

Evil One before he fell. No mention is made of this detail in subsequent reports; but in the Abbot's deposition the phrase *"Post annos novem"* is used, and the compiler also repeats *"ad novem annos"* in his summary, in itself a proof that the number was not regarded as unimportant.

The number Nine has become familiar to us in neurotic phantasies. Nine is the term of the months of gestation, and reference to the number Nine, whatever its connection, directs our attention to a phantasy of pregnancy. In this case, to be sure, the number refers to years, not to months, and it might be objected that the number can be of significance in other directions. But who can say whether much of the sacrosanctity of this number is not altogether due to its relation to pregnancy; the change from nine months to nine years need not throw dust in our eyes. Dreams have taught us how "unconscious mental activity" plays with numbers. If, for example, the number five occurs in a dream, this refers invariably to a five of significance in waking life; the five may refer, however, in reality to five years' difference in age or to a company of five people, and this will appear in the dream as five pieces of money or five pieces of fruit. That is to say, the number itself is retained but the denominator is changed in accordance with the demands of condensation and displacement. Nine years in a dream could easily represent nine months in reality. The numbers of waking life are played with by the dream-work in other ways, too, as when the latter shows a lordly disregard for cyphers, not treating them as numbers at all. Five dollars in a dream may stand for fifty, five hundred, five thousand of the dollars of reality.

Another detail in the relation between the painter and the Devil also has a sexual reference. As has already been mentioned, when he first sees the Devil the latter appears in the shape of an honest burgher. On the very next occasion, however, he has already become naked, is malformed and has two pairs of breasts. Now in all of the subsequent apparitions breasts appear, sometimes singly, sometimes multiplied. On one occasion only, in addition to these breasts, the Devil has a large penis ending as a serpent.

This stressing of female sexual characteristics by the introduction of great pendulous breasts (there is never any indication of the female genitalia) would appear to be an obvious contradiction of our assumption that the Devil was a father-substitute to the painter. Moreover, such a mode of representing the Devil is in itself quite unusual. Where devils are conceived of as a species, that is to say, where they appear in the numbers, there is nothing extraordinary about the representation of female devils: but that *the* Devil, that mighty personage the Lord of Hell, the Adversary of God, should appear in any other guise but as a male, a superman indeed, with horns, tail and penis-serpent, does not seem to me to have been recorded.

These two slight indications suggest the typical factors that conditioned the negative side of the painter's attitude to his father. What he is struggling against is the feminine attitude to the father, which culminates in the phantasy of bearing him a child (nine years). We know this form of resistance very well from our analyses, where it takes many remarkable forms during the transference and is exceedingly troublesome. In his mourning for the departed father, and its intensification of the longing for him, the long-since-repressed phantasy of a pregnancy is re-awakened in our painter, which he must then defend himself against by means of a neurosis and by denigrating the father.

But why does the father, now reduced to the status of Devil, exhibit one of the bodily signs of womanhood? Here is a point which would at first seem difficult to interpret: two explanations, however, present themselves, vying with each other but at the same time mutually compatible. The feminine attitude to the father became repressed as soon as the boy realized that his rivalry with the woman for the father's love implies the loss of his own male genital, that is to say, implies castration. Repudiation of the feminine attitude is therefore a result of the struggle to avoid castration; it regularly finds its most emphatic expression in the contrasting phantasy of castrating the father and turning *him* into a woman. Hence the Devil's breasts would represent a projection of the man's own femininity on to the father-substitute. The other explanation of these female appurtenances in the Devil is in terms of tenderness, not of hostility; it sees in this female shape an indication of a transference of infantile affection from the mother to the father. The suggestion is that there had previously been a strong mother-fixation, which would in itself account in part for the hostility towards the father. The large breasts constitute the positive sexual characteristic of the mother, even at a time when the child is not familiar with the negative sign of womanhood, the absence of the penis.[18]

If it is his struggle against accepting castration which makes it impossible for the painter to yield to his longing for the father, it becomes entirely comprehensible that he should turn to the image of the mother for help and salvation. This is why he declares that he can only be released from the Pact by the Holy Mother of God at Mariazell and that he obtained his freedom on the Mother's birthday (September 8). Naturally we shall never know whether September 24, the day on which the Pact was executed, was not determined in some similar way.

Amongst all the observations concerning the mental life of children which psychoanalysis has made, there is hardly one which sounds so repugnant and incredible to the normal adult as the boy's feminine attitude to the father and the phantasy of pregnancy derived from it. Only since Daniel Paul Schreber, Senatspräsident[19] in Saxony, published the history of his psychotic illness and almost complete recovery, have we been able to speak of such things unconcernedly and with no need to apologize.[20] We learn from this invaluable book that at somewhere about the age of fifty the President became absolutely convinced that God—who incidentally had many of the characteristics of

[18] Cf. *Eine Kindheitserinnerung des Leonardo da Vinci.*

[19] [A Judge presiding over a Division in an Appeal Court. —Trans.]

[20] D. P. Schreber, *Denkwürdigkeiten eines Nervenkranken,* 1903. Cf. also "Psychoanalytic Notes upon an Autobiographical Account of a Case of Paranoia," *Three Case Histories,* Collier Books edition BS 191V.

his father, the worthy physician Dr. Schreber—had formed the decision to castrate him and use him as a woman in order to produce a new race born from the spirit of Schreber. (His own marriage was childless.) In his revolt against this decision on the part of God, which seemed to him highly unjust and "contrary to the order of things," he fell ill with symptoms of paranoia which, however, in the course of time died away, leaving only a few traces behind. The gifted writer could scarcely have guessed that in chronicling his own case-history he had brought to light a typical pathogenic factor.

This revolt against castration or the feminine attitude Alfred Adler has torn out of its organic context, has connected in a superficial or inaccurate way with the will to power and has represented as an independent trend, the "masculine protest." A neurosis, however, can never arise except from a conflict between two tendencies; hence it is just as possible to regard the masculine protest as the cause of "all" neuroses as to regard the feminine attitude against which it protests as the cause. It is perfectly true that this masculine protest is a constant component of character-formation which in some cases plays a very large part, also that it manifests itself as a vigorous resistance during the analysis of neurotic men. Psychoanalysis has paid due attention to the masculine protest in connection with the castration-complex, but has not been able to represent it as an omnipotent or omnipresent factor in the neuroses. The most outstanding case of masculine protest, as regards manifest reactions and character-traits, which ever came to me for treatment, did so on account of an obsessional neurosis in which the unresolved conflict between a masculine and a feminine attitude (fear of and desire for castration) was quite plainly expressed. This patient, moreover, had developed masochistic phantasies which were entirely derived from the wish to experience castration; and he had even gone beyond these phantasies to actual gratification in perverse ways. The whole of his condition was—like the Adlerian theory itself—due to a repression and repudiation of early infantile love-fixations.

President Schreber's recovery took its start from his decision to abandon all opposition to his castration and to accommodate himself to the feminine rôle designed for him by God. Following upon this, he became calm and clear in his mind, was able himself to arrange his dismissal from the asylum, and led a normal life, with the exception that he devoted some hours every day to the cultivation of his womanliness, remaining convinced that it would gradually mature to the final achievement of God's purpose.

4. THE TWO PACTS

A remarkable detail in the history of our painter is the recorded circumstance that he made two separate Pacts with the Devil. The first of these, written in black ink, ran as follows:[21]

> I, Christoph Haitzmann, sign a deede and pledge myselfe to be vnto this lord euen as a sonne of his bodie for 9 yeares   1669 yeare

The second, written in blood, runs:

> Anno 1669 Christoph Haizmann I give my bonde and pledge myselfe vnto this Satan for to be vnto him euen as a sonne of his bodie and after 9 yeares to belong vnto him bodie and saule

The originals of both are said to have been in the archives at Mariazell when the *Trophaeum* was written, and both bear the date 1669.

I have already made frequent reference to both these Pacts and propose now to deal with them in greater detail, although in this connection the danger of magnifying trifles seems especially imminent.

It is unusual to find a man selling himself twice to the Devil in such a way that the second bond is substituted for

[21] [Cf. pp. 445-6 for original text of these documents.— Trans.]

the first without cancelling it. Perhaps to those who are more familiar with demonological material it may not seem so surprising. For my own part I could only regard it as something peculiar to this case, and my suspicions were aroused when I found that precisely on this point there was some lack of correspondence in the various accounts. Close examination of these points of divergence affords us, quite unexpectedly, a deeper understanding of this clinical history.

The simplest and clearest account we have is that contained in the introductory letter from the Pastor of Pottenbrunn. Here mention is made of one Pact only, written by the painter in blood nine years before, which was due to expire a few days later, on September 24, and must therefore have been written September 24, 1668; unfortunately this last date is not expressly mentioned, although one is entitled to make the deduction.

The deposition of the Abbot Franciscus, dated, as we know, a few days later (September 12, 1677), already describes a more complicated state of affairs. It is easy to assume that in the intervening period the painter had given more precise details. The deposition describes how the painter had made two Pacts, one in the year 1668 (a date which is in keeping with the Pastor's letter), written in black ink; the other, however, *sequenti anno 1669*, written in blood. It was this latter Pact, written in blood in 1669, which he received back on the Birthday of the Holy Virgin. This does not arise out of the Abbot's deposition, since it merely goes on to say: *schedam redderet* and *schedam sibi porrigentem conspexisset*, as if there could be only one document. It does follow, however, from the subsequent course of the story and from the coloured title-page of the *Trophaeum*, where one can plainly see *red* script on the bond held by the Dragon. As has already been mentioned, the subsequent events were that the painter returned to Mariazell in May 1678, having been once more tempted by the Evil One in Vienna, and begged that the Holy Mother would again have mercy upon him and cause the first Pact written in ink to be rendered up to him. How this came about is not so fully described as in the first instance; the report merely says *qua iuxta votum reddita*, and in another place the compiler states that this particular document was thrown to the painter by the Devil "all crumpled up and torn in four pieces"[22] on May 9, 1678, at nine o'clock in the evening.

Both Pacts, however, bear the same date: the year 1669.

This contradiction is either of no significance whatever, or else it affords us the following clue:

Starting from the Abbot's description, in which most details are given, we are faced with various difficulties. When Christoph Haitzmann informed the Pastor of Pottenbrunn that he was oppressed of the Devil and that the day of reckoning was at hand, he must have had in mind (in 1677) the Pact drawn up in the year 1668: that is to say, the first, black Pact (which in the introductory letter, by the way, is described as the only one and a blood Pact). In Mariazell a few days later, however, he is only concerned to get back the later blood Pact, which is not yet due to expire (1669–1677), thus allowing the first to become overdue. This latter is not reclaimed until 1678, *i.e.* when ten years have elapsed. We must ask further why both Pacts are dated in the same year 1669, in face of the fact that the report expressly attributes one to the "*anno subsequenti.*"

The compiler must have been aware of these difficulties, for he makes an attempt to smooth them out. In his preface he adopts the Abbot's version, but modifies it in one particular. The painter, he says, made an agreement in ink with the Devil in 1669, "*deinde vero,*" later, however, he made another in blood. He overrides the definite statement made in both reports that a Pact was concluded in 1668 and, in order to agree with the date written on both the returned Pacts, ignores the remark in the Abbot's deposition that there was a difference in date between the Pacts.

In the Abbot's deposition a paragraph appears in brackets following the words *sequenti vero anno 1669.*

[22] "*zusammengeknäult und in vier Stücke zerrissen.*"

This runs: *sumitur hic alter annus pro nondum completo uti saepe in loquendo fieri solet, nam eundum annum indicant Syngraphae quarum atramento scripta ante praesentem attestationem nondum habita fuit.* This is clearly an interpolation on the part of the compiler; since the Abbot, who had only seen one Pact, could not in any case have said that both bear the same date. The placing of this passage in brackets must have been intended to show that the paragraph was by a strange hand and not part of the Abbot's evidence. It is another attempt of the compiler to reconcile conflicting evidence. His view is that whilst it is indeed correct that the first Pact was drawn up in 1668, still the year was far advanced (September), hence the painter had postdated it by a year in order that both Pacts should bear the same date. His reference to a similar custom in contracts made by word of mouth may well stamp his whole attempt at reconciliation as an "idle prevarication."

Now I cannot tell whether my presentation of the case will have made any impression on the reader or whether it has aroused his interest sufficiently in such minutiae. For my own part, I found it impossible to explain the case in a manner which disposed of all doubt, but in the course of my study of the situation I ventured on a surmise which has the advantage of putting the events in the most natural order, even though the documentary evidence does not entirely cover it.

My view is that during his first visit to Mariazell the painter mentioned only one regular Pact, the one which was written in blood, was about to fall due and was drawn up on September 8, 1668, precisely as described by the Pastor in his introductory letter. In Mariazell also he produced this blood Pact as the one returned to him by the Devil under compulsion by the Holy Mother. We know what happened afterwards. The painter soon left Mariazell and went to Vienna, where until the middle of October he felt much better. Then, however, he again fell ill and the apparitions which he regarded as the work of the Evil One recommenced. He once more felt in need of redemption but was faced with the difficulty of explaining why the exorcism in the Holy Shrine had not brought about permanent relief. Returning merely as a relapsed case, he could scarcely have been welcome at Mariazell. To overcome this difficulty he invented a previous Pact, which, however, should be written in ink, so that its relative insignificance in comparison with the later blood Pact might seem more plausible. Once more at Mariazell, he brought about the return of this alleged first Pact also. Then he was at last freed from the attentions of the Evil One, though he immediately did something else which serves to indicate to us what was underlying his neurosis.

The drawings he made were certainly executed on the occasion of his second sojourn at Mariazell: the title-page is of one piece and represents both Pact scenes. The attempt to make his fresh account tally with the earlier story may well have occasioned him some embarrassment. Clearly it was inconvenient that he could only invent an earlier Pact instead of a later one. So he could not avoid the awkward result that he had redeemed the one blood Pact too soon (in the eighth year) and the other black Pact too late (in the tenth year). It then happened that in dating the Pacts he blunders, making the earlier one, too, date from the year 1669, thus betraying by this sign his twofold editing of the story. This blunder may be regarded as a piece of unintentional honesty: it enables us to guess that the alleged earlier Pact was actually fabricated at a later date. The compiler, whose work was carried out certainly not before 1714 and perhaps not till 1729, was faced with the necessity of explaining away, as best he could, this conflicting evidence about details that were far from unimportant. Finding that both the Pacts in his possession were dated 1669, he had recourse to a subterfuge, the terms of which are interpolated in the Abbot's deposition.

We can easily see wherein the weakness of this otherwise engaging speculation lies. In the Abbot's deposition reference is already made to the existence of two Pacts, one black and the other written in blood. Hence I am faced with the alternative either of insinuating that the compiler here tampered with the deposition itself, in order to make it tally with his interpolated paragraph, or of admitting frankly that I cannot unravel the tangle.[23]

I daresay the reader will consider all this discussion as superfluous and regard the issues themselves as quite too trivial. Nevertheless, if we follow the matter up in a certain direction, it will be found to acquire fresh interest.

I have already expressed my opinion that, when the painter was disagreeably overtaken by a recurrence of his illness, he invented an earlier Pact (in ink) in order to put himself right with the fathers at Mariazell. Now since I write for those who believe in psychoanalysis and not in the Devil, my readers could point out how absurd it is to bring such an accusation against the poor fellow—*hunc miserum* he is called in the introductory letter. For the blood Pact, they might say, was just as much a product of phantasy as the alleged earlier Pact written in ink. The Devil never appeared to the painter in reality at all, and the whole Satanic Pact existed only in his imagination. I quite realize this: one cannot deny the poor fellow the right to supplement his original phantasy with a new one when occasion demands.

But the matter cannot be allowed to rest here. Unlike the apparitions of the Evil One, the two Pacts are by no

[23] In my opinion the compiler found himself on the horns of a dilemma. On the one hand, he discovered that, not only in the Pastor's introductory letter but in the Abbot's deposition, the Pact (at all events, the first one) is described as having been made in 1668; on the other hand, both Pacts preserved in the archives bore the date 1669. That two Pacts lay before him was, in his view, conclusive evidence that two had been made. Since, however, as I believe, there was mention in the Abbot's deposition of only one Pact, he felt impelled to insert in the deposition some reference to the existence of another, subsequently reconciling any contradiction by his assumption of post-dating. This textual alteration occurs immediately before the interpolated paragraph which he alone could have inserted. He was compelled to link up this para-

means products of phantasy; they were documents which, according to the assurance of the copyist and of the deposition of the Abbot Kilian, were preserved in the archives at Mariazell where they could be seen and handled by all and sundry. We are therefore in a dilemma. Either we must assume that the painter himself drew up, at the time when he stood in need of them, both the *Schedae* which he alleged were returned to him by the grace of God, or else we must, despite all solemn assurances, sealed testimony of witnesses and so on, discount the credibility of the ecclesiastics of Mariazell and St. Lambert. I must admit I am not inclined to take the latter course. To be sure, I incline to the view that the compiler, in the interests of conformity, has falsified part of the deposition of the first Abbot, but this "secondary elaboration" does not much exceed what is quite commonly perpetrated in this direction even by lay modern historians, and at all events it was done in good faith. In other ways these reverend fathers have established good claim on our credence. As I said before, there was nothing to prevent their suppressing the accounts of the incomplete nature of the cure and the recurrence of temptation by the Evil One: moreover, the description of the redemption-scenes in the shrine, about which one might have some anticipatory apprehensions, is

---

graph to the textual alteration with the words *sequenti vero anno* 1669, since the painter had expressly written under the (much damaged) title-page illustrations:

> Nach einem Jahr würdt Er
> .   . schrökhliche betrohungen in ab-
> .   .   gestalt Nr. 2 bezwungen sich,
> .   .   .   n Bluut zu verschreiben.
>
> (A year after He was
> .   .   .   horrid threatenings by the
> .   .   .   . shape No. 2 compelled
> .   .   .   to give a Pact in Bloode.)

The blunder made by the painter in writing his Syngraphae, which induced me to bring forward this attempt at explanation, appears to me to be no less interesting a product of his pen than the Pacts themselves.

in fact soberly given and inspires confidence. So there is nothing for it but to lay the accusation at the painter's door. The blood Pact he probably already had with him when he went to the shrine for the penitential prayer, and he produced it when he came back to the assembled company after his meeting with the Evil One. Moreover, this need not have been the same document that was afterwards preserved in the archives, but in accordance with our surmise may have borne the date 1668 (nine years before the exorcism).

5. SUBSEQUENT COURSE OF THE NEUROSIS

But then it would all have been a ruse rather than a neurosis, the painter a malingerer and a cheat instead of a man sick of demoniacal possession! But the transition-stages between neurosis and malingering are, as we know, very elastic. Nor do I see any difficulty in assuming that the painter manufactured this Pact—and the later one too—and took it with him in a state comparable to that during which he saw his visions. Indeed, there was no other course open to him if he wished to realize his phantasy of a Pact with Satan and of a subsequent redemption.

The Diary written in Vienna, however, which he gave to the priests on the occasion of his second visit to Mariazell, bears the stamp of veracity. It certainly affords us deeper insight into the motivation, or we will say rather, the utilization of the neurosis.

The entries date from his successful redemption until January 13 of the following year, 1678. Until October 11 he did very well in Vienna, where he lived with a married sister, but from that date he was taken with fresh seizures accompanied by visions, convulsions, loss of consciousness and painful sensations, which ultimately led to his return to Mariazell in May 1678.

This relapse can be divided into three phases. First of all temptation comes in the form of a gaily dressed cavalier, who tries to induce him to part with the document attesting his admission to the Brotherhood of the Holy Rosary. This temptation is successfully withstood, only to be repeated on the following day; the scene is laid in a marvellously decorated hall where high-born men are dancing with beautiful women. The same cavalier makes a proposal to him concerning painting,[24] promising him in return a goodly sum of money. With prayer this vision is overcome, but it is repeated a few days later in a more pressing form. On this occasion the cavalier sends one of the most beautiful of the ladies sitting at the banquet-table to persuade the painter to mingle with them, and he has some difficulty in defending himself from the wiles of the fair seducer. Most terrifying of all was the vision which occurred shortly afterwards; it took place in a still more magnificent hall in which there stood a throne "built verie high with pieces of golde,"[25] near which the courtiers awaited the arrival of their king. The same person who had so often importuned him now came forward and begged the painter to ascend the throne, for they "would have him for to be their King, to honour him for ever and aye."[26] This elaboration of his phantasy concludes the first, and entirely perspicuous, phase of the story of his temptation.

A reaction was now inevitable; asceticism came to the fore. On October 20 a great light appeared to him, from which came the voice of Christ commanding him to forswear this wicked world and to serve God in a desert for a period of six years. The painter clearly suffered more from these holy visions than from the earlier devilish apparitions; he came out of this seizure only after two and a half hours. On the next occasion the sacred figure enveloped in light was much more hostile, upbraided him for neglecting to obey the sacred behest, and led him into Hell that he might be duly terrified by the fate of the damned. Evidently, however, this had not the required effect, since visions of a Being enveloped in light who was supposed to be Christ recurred several times after, each

[24] This part is unintelligible to me.
[25] *Ein von "Goldstuckh aufgerichteter Thron."*
[26] *"Wollten ihn für ihren König halten und in Ewigkeit verehren."*

seizure being accompanied by a loss of consciousness lasting some hours and by a state of ecstasy. During the most
impressive of all these ecstasies, this Being led him first of
all into a town whose inhabitants performed all the works
of darkness in the streets, and then for contrast to quiet
pastures wherein hermits led a godly life and received
tangible evidence of the grace and goodness of God. There
then appeared, instead of Christ, the Holy Mother herself,
who reminded the painter of what she had already done
on his behalf and called on him to obey Her Beloved Son's
behests. "Since he coulde not resolue so to doe,"[27] Christ
reappeared to him on the following day, rebuked him
roundly and endeavoured to prevail on him with promises.
Then at last he gave way, made up his mind to leave the
world and to do what was required of him. The second
phase ends with this decision. The painter states that from
this time onward he saw no more apparitions and was
never again tempted.

Nevertheless, his resolution cannot have been very
strong or he must have delayed too long in carrying it
out, since in the midst of his devotions on December 26,
in St. Stephen's, he caught sight of a strapping wench
accompanied by a well-dressed man and could not help
thinking that he might have filled the latter's shoes. On the
same evening, like a bolt from the blue, punishment was
meted out; he saw the flames swallowing him up and fell
in a swoon. Attempts were made to rouse him, but he
grovelled in the room till blood flowed from his nose and
mouth; he became aware of the scorching heat and the foul
fumes, and heard a voice declaring that this was the punishment for his vain and unprofitable thoughts. Later he was
scourged by evil spirits with ropes and informed that the
punishment would be repeated every day until he decided
to enter the order of anchorites. These experiences continued up to the last entry (January 13).

We see how our unfortunate painter's phantasies of
temptation were succeeded by ascetic ones and finally by

[27] *"Da er sich hiezu nicht recht resolviret."*

those of punishment; the end we know already. In May he went to Mariazell, told the story of an earlier Pact written in black ink, to which he evidently ascribed his continued temptation by the Devil, received back this Pact and was finally healed.

During this second sojourn there he painted the pictures which are copied in the *Trophaeum*; next, however, he took a step which was in accord with the demands of the ascetic phase described in his Diary. To be sure, he did not go into the desert to live as a hermit but he joined the Order of Monks Hospitallers: *religiosus factus est.*

Perusal of the Diary gives us insight into another part of the narrative. We remember that the painter pledges himself to the Evil One because after his father's death he feels depressed, incapable of work and is apprehensive about his livelihood. These factors, depression, lack of working capacity and grief, have some connection with one another, whether it be a simple or a complex one. Perhaps the Devil is furnished so generously with breasts because he is to become a foster-father. This hope not being realized, the patient's condition deteriorated; he could not work properly, or perhaps he was out of luck and had not sufficient work to do. The Pastor's introductory letter speaks of him as *"hunc miserum omni auxilio destitutum."* He was thus not only in moral straits, he was literally in want. In the account of his later visions we find here and there remarks indicating, like the content of the scenes portrayed, that even after the first successful redemption nothing of this had changed. We come to realize that he was of the type which cannot make its way in the world and which inspires confidence in no one. In the first vision the cavalier asks him what he is going to do, since nobody takes any interest in him.[28] The first series of phantasies in Vienna corresponds entirely with the wish-phantasies of the poverty-stricken, of such as have come down in the world and hunger after pleasure: magnificent halls, high

---

[28] *"Dieweillen ich von iedermann izt verlassen, wass ich anfangen würde."*

living, silver-ware and lovely women; here we find what was missing in his traffic with the Devil. At that time he had been in the depths of a melancholia which caused him to turn from all enjoyment and to ignore the most tempting offers. After his redemption the melancholia seems to have been overcome and all the longings of a worldling rise up once more.

In one of the ascetic visions he complains to his guide (Christ) that nobody has any faith in him, hence that he is unable to carry out the commands laid upon him. The reply given is unfortunately obscure. "So inasmuch as they will not beleeve me yet doe I know well what has happened but am vnapt to speak a worde about it."[29] On the other hand, what happens when the celestial guide takes him amongst the hermits is very enlightening. He comes to a cave in which an old man has been sitting for the last sixty years; in answer to his question he is told that an angel from Heaven feeds this old man every day. He then sees for himself an angel bringing food: "Three pannikins with food, one of bread, one of dumpling and wherewithall to drink."[30] After the hermit has fed, the angel collects everything and carries it away. We realize from this the nature of the temptations presented in the pious visions: he is to be induced to adopt a mode of life in which there are no cares about sustenance. The utterances of Christ in the last vision are also worthy of note. After the threat that, should he not prove more amenable, something would come to pass (which) both he and the people would be bound (to) believe, he says directly that "I should not heed the people even if they would persecute me or give me no succour, God would not forsake me."[31]

Christoph Haitzmann was enough of an artist and a

[29] "So fer man mir nit glauben, wass aber geschechen, waiss ich wol, ist mir aber selbes auszuspröchen unmöglich."

[30] "Drei Schüsserl mit Speiss, ein Brot und ein Knödl und Getränk."

[31] "Ich solle die Leith nit achten, obwollen ich von ihnen verfolgt wurdte, oder von ihnen keine hilfflaistung empfienge, Gott würde mich nit verlassen."

worldling to find it difficult to renounce this sinful world. Nevertheless, he did so in the end, because of the helplessness of his position. He entered a holy order, where his inner conflict as well as his material want came to an end. This outcome is reflected in the neurosis by the return of the alleged earlier Pact that puts an end to his attacks and visions. Actually, both stages of his demonological illness had the same signification. All he wanted was security in life, at first with the help of Satan but at the cost of eternal bliss; then, when this failed and had to be abandoned, with the Church's help but at the cost of his freedom and most of the pleasures of life. Perhaps Christoph Haitzmann was only a poor devil, one of those who never have any luck; perhaps he was too poorly gifted, too ineffective to make a living, and belonged to that well-known type, the "eternal suckling"—to those who are unable to tear themselves away from the joyous haven at the mother's breast, who hold fast all through their lives to their claim to be nourished by someone else. And so in his illness our painter followed the path from his own father by way of the Devil as a father-substitute to the pious Fathers.

To superficial observation his neurosis looks like a sort of jugglery covering some part of the very serious, if banal, anxiety of the struggle for existence. This aspect of it is not, of course, an invariable one, but it is by no means rare. In analytical experience we frequently find how unsatisfactory it is to treat a business man who "in other respects healthy, has for some time shown signs of a neurosis." The catastrophe which he knows to be threatening his business induces the neurosis as a by-product, with the advantage that behind the symptoms the man is able to conceal his real apprehensions about his livelihood. In every other respect, however, it is more than inexpedient, since it uses up energies which would be more advantageously applied in handling the threatening situation with all possible skill.

In a far greater number of cases the neurosis is more of a thing apart, more independent of the claims of self-preservation and maintenance. The interests at stake in the conflict giving rise to neurosis are either purely libidinal, or have a close libidinal relation to those of self-preservation. In all three instances the dynamics of the neurosis are identical. Libido, dammed up and unable to secure real gratification, finds discharge through the repressed unconscious by the help of regression to old fixations. In so far as the patient's ego can extract from this process a paranosic or epinosic gain, it countenances the neurosis, although there can be no manner of doubt about the economic handicap it signifies.

Not even our painter's wretched situation in life would have induced his neurosis of demoniacal possession, had not his material necessities served to intensify a longing for his father. After his melancholia and his relations with the Devil had been played out, there still remained the conflict between his libidinal pleasure in life and his recognition that in the interests of self-preservation he must become a stern anchorite and ascetic. It is interesting to see that the painter was well aware of the identity behind the two phases of his illness, since he attributed both the one and the other to Pacts which he had delivered to the Devil. On the other hand, he draws no sharp distinction between the machinations of the Evil One and those of Heavenly Powers; he had but one characterization for both—manifestations of the Devil.